Clovelly harbour from the Hobby Drive.

Shire County Guide 27

DEVON

Peter Stanier

Shire Publications Ltd

CONTENTS

1. Glorious Devon 3
2. Coast and country 12
3. Places of archaeological interest 19
4. Castles and coastal fortifications 25
5. Churches 31
6. Historic buildings and gardens 38
7. Museums and art galleries 50
8. Industrial archaeology 59
9. Other places to visit 65
10. Towns and villages 71
    Maps of Devon 92
    Index 96

Printed in Great Britain by C. I. Thomas & Sons (Haverfordwest) Ltd, Press Buildings, Merlins Bridge, Haverfordwest, Dyfed SA61 1XF.

British Library Cataloguing in Publication Data: Stanier, Peter. Devon. — (Shire county guide; 27). 1. Devon — Visitors' guides. I. Title. 914. 23'504858. ISBN 0-85263-983-X.

ACKNOWLEDGEMENTS
Photographs are acknowledged as follows: Janice Johns, pages 47, 64 (top), 86; HMS Osprey and the Warship Preservation Trust, page 69; Peter Stanier, pages 5, 12, 19, 22, 23, 25, 26, 27 (right), 29, 32, 33, 34, 35, 36, 38, 39, 43, 44, 52, 53, 58, 60, 62, 64 (bottom), 65, 73, 74, 77, 78, 79 (top), 80, 83. All others, including the front cover, are by Cadbury Lamb. The maps are by Robert Dizon.

Cover: *The clapper bridge at Postbridge on Dartmoor.*

Below: *Totnes, with the castle in the background.*

Widecombe-in-the-Moor.

1
Glorious Devon

Devon is the third largest county in England, after North Yorkshire and Cumbria, yet its population almost equals their combined totals. It borders Cornwall on the west and Somerset and Dorset on the east and is unique among the English counties in that it has two distinctly separate coastlines: north and south. Devon has the highest land in southern England, rising to over 2000 feet (610 metres) on Dartmoor. The major centres of population are in the south, at Plymouth, Torbay and Exeter. Although smaller than Plymouth, Exeter is well served by communications and is the administrative centre for the county. Apart from these and Barnstaple in the north, Devon communities consist mostly of scattered market towns and villages.

The interesting and varied geology of Devon creates distinct regions with rewarding inland and coastal scenery. Central Devon is dominated by the high mass of Dartmoor, a rugged wilderness which is deservedly a National Park. Craggy granite is sometimes exposed but was intruded into different rocks. These are mainly Devonian shales and slates, with some limestone in the south, and grits and sandstones in the far north. Here Devon claims a second National Park: a portion of Exmoor lies within this corner of the county. The so-called Culm measures of the Carboniferous period lie across north Devon between Exmoor and Dartmoor. Around Exeter, the New Red Sandstones give the famous red soils of Devon. Further east, the plateau surfaces and escarpments are of the younger Cretaceous greensands, with chalk cliffs at Beer Head and along the coast into Dorset. Among more recent deposits, boulder clays around the Taw estuary indicate that glaciers touched Devon's north coast during the ice age.

The landscape has been dissected by rivers and their tributaries, mostly flowing to the south. The source of the Tamar is close to the north coast, and for much of its southerly course it forms the border with Cornwall before emerging at Plymouth Sound. The Exe rises on Exmoor (actually within Somerset) and passes through a wooded valley and gentler country until it broadens into a wide estuary south of Exeter. The most important Dartmoor rivers, such as the Avon, Dart, Erme, Plym, Tavy and Teign, all form deep estuaries or rias which indent the south coast. The Axe, Culm and Otter flow south in gentler vales through the softer rocks of east Devon. The Taw and Okement are the only significant rivers which flow northwards from Dartmoor. The other great north Devon river, the Torridge, doubles back on itself after starting near the coast on the Hartland peninsula. The Taw and Torridge join at the only estuary on this Atlantic coast, which is otherwise characterised by high cliffs and sweeping bays. The short but infamous West and East Lyn rivers flow north from Exmoor. The granite island of Lundy is 12 miles (19 km) off Hartland Point,

3

The sand dunes at Woolacombe.

at the gateway to the Bristol Channel.

The influence of the sea brings a generally mild climate, but the changes in altitude produce great contrasts. Torbay's climate has earned it the name of the English Riviera and sub-tropical plants can grow here, yet just a few miles away there can be almost arctic conditions on the more exposed and higher parts of Dartmoor. Blizzards are experienced here in winter and drifting snow may cut off remote farms and villages for days. Rainfall can be high on Dartmoor, with over 100 inches (2550 mm) recorded at Princetown.

Into this varied landscape came prehistoric man, but it is Dartmoor which dominates the archaeological map, with its magnificent hut-circles, field systems, stone rows and circles. Almost undisturbed since they were abandoned, they are evidence of a kinder climate which allowed colonisation of the moor in the bronze age. Devon has its share of iron age hillforts, while the Romans established their only major centre at Exeter, where parts of the much repaired town wall survive.

Place-names suggest widespread Saxon set tlement of the countryside. Exeter was a key town and was occupied in the seventh century, while King Ine's victory near Lifton in AD 710 seems to have secured most of the county. Skirmishes with the Danes also played a part in the early history of Devon. Exeter was occupied by Guthrum over the winter of AD 876-7, and to meet this threat Saxon *burhs* were created in the following year at Exeter, Halwell, Lydford and Pilton. In AD 997 Lydford repulsed an attack by the Danes who roamed inland and destroyed the recently founded abbey at Tavistock. In AD 1001 they plundered the lower Teign area, and two years later they again occupied and sacked Exeter. Later Gwytha, mother of Harold, fled with her daughter to Exeter, where William the Conqueror laid siege for eighteen days. William commissioned the castle here, but little more than the gateway now remains. Berry Pomeroy, Lydford, Okehampton and Totnes are among the best castles to survive, but there are several motte and bailey earthworks around the county.

Crediton had a bishop and cathedral between AD 909 and 1050, before the see was removed to Exeter, where the cathedral is among the finest in England. There were bishop's palaces at Paignton and Bishopsteignton, of which some traces remain. Crediton became an important collegiate church, as did Ottery St Mary. There were already two Benedictine monasteries in Devon in late Saxon times, at Tavistock and Buckfast. The latter was taken over by the Cistercians, who developed sheep farming on the edges of Dartmoor. They also had the important Forde Abbey (now in Dorset) and founded Buckland Abbey in 1278, the last in Devon. The Augustinians founded Plympton (1121) and Hartland (1170). Barnstaple was the most important Cluniac house in Devon, but like the others it was dependent on outside abbeys.

4

At the time of the Dissolution the three richest abbeys were Plympton, Tavistock and Buckfast. Buckland and Torre abbeys became private residences and still survive. The Prayer Book Rebellion of 1549 began and ended at Sampford Courtenay, but not before a five-week siege of Exeter was lifted by Lord Russell and his brutal mercenaries.

The sea has always played an important part in the economy and way of life of Devon. This was especially so in Elizabethan times, when Devon produced some of the most famous names in maritime history. Sir Francis Drake (c. 1540-96) was born at Tavistock and is best known for his voyage around the world in 1577-80 and his part in the defeat of the Spanish Armada in 1588. He settled at Buckland Abbey and supervised a number of improvements to Plymouth: a castle and a leat to supply fresh water from Dartmoor. Sir John Hawkins from Plymouth was the first Englishman in the slave trade and was knighted for his action against the Armada. Sir Walter Raleigh was born at Hayes Barton near East Budleigh. His half-brother, Sir Humphrey Gilbert of Compton Castle, claimed Newfoundland for England in 1583. Another great Devon navigator of this period was John Davis, who searched for the North-West Passage and gave his name to the Davis Strait between Greenland and Baffin Island.

There were minor skirmishes in the following century as Civil War armies passed through Devon to and from strongly Royalist Cornwall. Barnstaple changed hands four times in as many years, and Tavistock six, but the most important event in the county was the great siege of Plymouth, which remained in Parliamentarian hands throughout the Civil War. Great defensive works were set up around the town, which continued to be reinforced and replenished by sea. It was at Brixham that William of Orange stepped ashore in December 1688 before travelling overland to Exeter; his baggage was landed at Topsham. Napoleon saw the English shore as a prisoner from the deck of HMS *Bellerophon* anchored off Brixham in 1815. He had a second taste of Devon when his ship put into Plymouth Sound.

Devon has had its share of famous artists and writers. For example, Sir Joshua Reynolds was born at Plympton, and the miniaturist Richard Cosway came from Tiverton. The poet Samuel Taylor Coleridge was born at Ottery St Mary, where his father was the vicar and schoolmaster. Charles Kingsley was born at picturesque Holne on the edge of Dartmoor, and although he lived for much of his life in Hampshire his book *Westward Ho!* stemmed from his boyhood in Devon. The Reverend Sabine Baring-Gould of Lewtrenchard is best known for his hymn 'Onward Christian Soldiers' but was also a writer and archaeologist. More recently Henry Williamson lived in north Devon, the inspiration for his famous book *Tarka the Otter*, while Agatha Christie was born at Torquay and made her home near the banks of the Dart in south Devon.

Farming is a traditional occupation. In medieval times wool from local sheep established a rich woollen and cloth industry which continued to bring wealth to centres such as Tiverton and Exeter until the eighteenth century. There are hardy Dartmoor and Exmoor sheep breeds and the county has its own South Devon cattle. On the moorlands sheep, cattle and ponies are all grazed from hill farms, while dairying is important in the richer lowlands. There are important dairies and creameries throughout Devon and some, such as at Totnes, were established next to the main railway to London. The rich red soils of Devon produce arable crops, while cidermaking in the east is nationally famous. River and estuary fishing for salmon has been important in the

One of the few remaining parts of Tavistock Abbey.

Sir Walter Raleigh's birthplace, Hayes Barton near East Budleigh.

great rivers such as the Exe, Dart, Taw, Torridge and Tamar.

The medieval tin industry on Dartmoor made this the major producing district of Europe. As in Cornwall it came under the jurisdiction of the Stannaries with its own parliament and courts. The tinners' parliament was held at Crockern Tor near Two Bridges, and Lydford had a notorious jail for offenders. Tax on smelted tin was paid at the coinage towns of Ashburton, Chagford, Plympton and Tavistock. Other minerals such as copper, iron, lead and manganese have been mined around the flanks of Dartmoor and near North Molton. Silver too was mined at Combe Martin. The greatest copper mine in Europe during the second half of the nineteenth century was Devon Great Consols in the important mining district around Tavistock. Wolfram (tungsten) has been extracted by open-cast methods at Hemerdon near Plymouth, where large-scale working of an extensive ore body has been proposed. Nearby Lee Moor has huge excavations of china clay on the very edge of Dartmoor, and small disused pits lie elsewhere. Important deposits of ball clay are mined around Bovey Tracey and Petrockstow.

Before good inland communications, the twin coasts and their estuaries were worked by hundreds of small sailing craft. The Tamar, Teign and Taw-Torridge estuaries had their own sailing barges plying a busy trade. Exeter has an early ship canal, built in 1566 and subsequently enlarged on several occasions. In the nineteenth century, ports like Dartmouth and Salcombe had fleets of schooners which traded to the rest of Britain, the Mediterranean and across the Atlantic. In north Devon,

Bideford and Barnstaple were once thriving ports. Appledore was also an important shipping centre, and shipbuilding is still carried on at a modern yard, which is a major employer in the district. Brixham and Plymouth are the important centres for sea-fishing, the former having once been Britain's premier trawling port.

A naval tradition was strengthened by the establishment of a dockyard at Plymouth Dock (later Devonport). This was greatly expanded in the nineteenth century to become the largest naval base in western Europe. Rennie's long breakwater made Plymouth Sound a good anchorage for naval and commercial vessels. Until the 1960s transatlantic liners called to land mails and passengers, who continued to London on special boat trains. More recently the Sound has been frequented by smaller craft: sailing championships, transatlantic and round-the-world yachtsmen, and as the finishing point of the Fastnet Race.

The tourist industry in Devon originated in seaside resorts such as Exmouth, Sidmouth and Torquay which were fashionable during the Napoleonic Wars. This has continued with the aid of improved road and rail links with the rest of England. The first railway was the Bristol and Exeter, opened in 1844 and continued as the South Devon Railway to Plymouth four years later. Brunel engineered the difficult section along the coast at Dawlish and the hilly country between Newton Abbot and Plymouth. He also experimented with an atmospheric railway along the coastal section from Exeter to Newton Abbot. The whole line became part of the Great Western Railway in 1876. The rival London and South Western Railway from Waterloo did not reach Exeter until 1860 and Plymouth in 1890. The continuation of this line around the north of Dartmoor, through Okehampton and Tavistock, enabled London trains to enter Plymouth from the west! Barnstaple was served by branches from Exeter and Taunton, but only the former survives. The railway branches played an important part in the development of resorts such as Ilfracombe, Paignton, Torquay, Sidmouth and Seaton.

Tourism developed further with the advent of the motor car, which gave access not just to the resorts but to the delights of the Devon countryside and its villages. The days of peak bank-holiday traffic jams on the Exeter bypass are now gone, and Devon is well served by the M5 motorway, bringing the county within easy reach of Bristol and the Midlands. Improvements to the A30 and A38 have relieved congestion further west, while the North Devon Link is opening up the north. These are the main arteries, but Devon has around 8000 miles (12,800 km) of roads, the greatest mileage of any county in England. Many are tiny sunken lanes cut from the solid rock.

DARTMOOR

Dartmoor is one of the last great wildernesses of southern England. It is granite upland mostly over 700 feet (213 metres) and up to 2000 feet (610 metres) in the north. In 1951 all the granite and part of the surrounding area was designated a National Park of 365 square miles (945 sq km). A dome of granite was intruded beneath older rocks about 280 million years ago and has been since exposed

by erosion. There are coarse and finer-grained types, the former making up the characteristic tors on summits and spurs in parts of the moor. The great tors have been weathered out of the granite around the vertical and horizontal jointing system. Major landmarks and popular visiting spots include Haytor and Houndtor in the south-east, Belstone Tor, High Willhays and Yes Tor in the north, and Pew Tor and Staple Tor in the west.

Past erosion surfaces have given the high moor a plateau-like appearance and the open moors offer no shelter. Large areas are covered with blanket bog, making walking difficult and hazardous in poor conditions. Vegetation includes purple moor grass, bog cotton, heathers, bracken and whortleberry. The practice of swaling or burning encourages new growth for grazing. There are three relict woodlands of importance — Wistman's Wood, Black Tor Beare and Piles Copse — where stunted oaks grow among rocks covered with ferns, lichens and mosses.

Most river drainage radiates from the high moor in the north. The Plym, East and West Dart, Teign, Erme, Tavy and Avon all have long courses to the south, while the north-flowing East and West Okement and Taw soon leave Dartmoor. The Dart and Teign once flowed east and retain sections in that direction. There are beauty spots around the edge of the moor, where rivers descend steep wooded valleys such as at the Dewerstone, Fingle Bridge, Lustleigh Cleave and Lydford Gorge. In contrast Tavy Cleave is open, a great cleft between rocky tors as the river breaks out from the moorland interior. Man

Dartmoor ponies.

has enhanced the scene with clapper and arched bridges, which are popular stopping places for visitors. In late Victorian and Edwardian times the remoter wooded rocky places were popular, such as at Lustleigh Cleave and around Chagford. Guides were available to escort visitors, one well known figure being James Perrott of Chagford. Others such as William Crossing and R. H. Worth have done much to publicise the moor with the publication of guide books.

While sunny days bring out the colours of the moor, the climate can also be appalling with rapidly changing conditions bringing fog, low cloud and heavy rainfall. Princetown, at 1358 feet (414 metres), has an average of 82 inches (2083 mm) per year, compared with 35 inches (889 mm) at Torquay. Snowfall can be heavy and may lie for over thirty days a year on the exposed summits. Roads and isolated farms are frequently cut off by drifts.

Man has exploited Dartmoor since at least early bronze age times, and archaeological remains show evidence for extensive settlement and farming with additional ritual monuments. The climate was more agreeable then to allow this colonisation of the moor, but the growth of peat covering some of these sites is clear evidence of a subsequent deterioration. These people may have been tin streamers, but it was not until medieval times that the Dartmoor tin industry became the most productive in Europe. As with the lead miners of Derbyshire, the tinners had their own courts, laws and parliament. A jail was built at Lydford and stannary towns were established at Ashburton, Chagford and Tavistock, with a fourth added at Plympton. From the early fourteenth century coinage dues were paid to the Duke of Cornwall on all tin smelted and sold at these towns. The boundaries of the coinage towns met at Crockern Tor, where was held, rather intermittently, the Great Court or Parliament. This was called by the Warden, who summoned 24 representatives from each district. The coinage dues were abolished in 1838 (the last took place at Morwellham) and the stannary courts in 1896.

Dartmoor has been exploited for its minerals down to the present day. Tin was also mined, the last activity being at Birch Tor and Vitifer in 1926. There have been other mines around the fringes of the moor. The largest project is at Hemerdon Ball near Plymouth, where an open-cast scheme would create the largest tungsten mine in Europe. The surface boulders or 'moorstones' were used for local building purposes for centuries, but granite quarrying did not develop until the nineteenth century. The largest quarries were at Haytor (producing stone for London Bridge and other buildings in the capital) and Foggintor (from which came Nelson's Column). The only quarry still working is at Merrivale, which has operated for over a hundred years. The largest china-clay workings on Dartmoor are at Lee Moor near Plymouth, developed after 1833 by William Phillips, who built the Lee Moor Tramway, workers' cottages and a porcelain works. The tramway is now closed as clay is piped to a drying plant at Marsh Mills. Small china-clay pits were worked at Redlake and

The graves of former Dartmoor prisoners in the churchyard at Princetown.

served by a tramway from near Ivybridge.

The fringes and some lower valleys of the moor have been enclosed for farming, while sheep, cattle and ponies are grazed out on the open moorland. Forestry has played an increasing part in the local economy since the First World War, with notable plantations of conifers at Fernworthy and Bellever. Valleys on the east side of the moor have more mixed deciduous forest. Peat-cutting rights have existed since a charter of Henry III. There were several attempts to extract naphtha from peat but the remoteness of Dartmoor prevented any real success. Projects at Zeal Tor and Omen Beam had tramways, while Rattlebrook had a siding from the London and South Western Railway at Bridestowe. This latter worked intermittently carrying naphtha and horticultural peat until the mid 1950s.

The infamous Dartmoor prison was begun by Thomas Tyrwhitt on his Tor Royal estate at Princetown in 1806. It was used for French and American prisoners of war in the period 1809-16 but then remained empty until becoming a convict prison in 1850. Tyrwhitt's other plan was to open a railway to exploit the peat, agriculture and granite of this part of Dartmoor, but only the granite provided a trade for the Plymouth and Dartmoor Railway.

Another natural asset exploited was water supply. This began as early as 1591 with the opening of Drake's 17 mile (27 km) Plymouth Leat from the Meavy near Sheepstor. Two hundred years later the Plymouth Dock Waterworks Company was given powers to build a new leat from the West Dart to what was to become Devonport. The works included a tunnel near Whiteworks. Early in the twentieth century the leat was diverted to Plymouth's newly constructed Burrator Reservoir, which it still feeds. The disused lower course can be seen alongside Drake's leat crossing Roborough Down. Other reservoirs include Venford (1907) and Fernworthy (1936-42), supplying Paignton and Torquay. The attractive finger-like reservoirs of Kennick, Tottiford and Trenchford are on the east of the moor, and the Avon Dam is in the south. The last major dam to be built was the Meldon Reservoir on the West Okement in the 1970s. In the same period a £14 million scheme to flood 760 acres (307 ha) at Swincombe for Plymouth's water supply was rejected, but the Roadford Reservoir of a similar size is due to be completed off the moor west of Okehampton in 1990. Dartmoor rivers and leats also supply small hydro-electric stations at Chagford, Mary Tavy and Morwellham.

Military training for the army and marines has taken place over large areas of Dartmoor since at least 1873. There is a training camp above Okehampton and the wilder parts of this north moor are used for training with live ammunition. The public are warned of times of live firing but allowed access at other times.

Dartmoor is a great resource for outdoor recreation and the moor is popular with walkers. A system of 'letter boxes' at many tors has developed, the first being a bottle for cards placed at the remote Cranmere Pool by James Perrott in 1854. The Ten Tors expedition is now an organised annual event involving hundreds of young people over a weekend period. An Outward Bound centre at Ashburton and other outdoor centres provide facilities for walking, climbing and canoeing. Rock climbing is possible on all the tors, although the Dewerstone and Haytor rocks provide the best. White-water canoeing is popular on some of the rivers as they descend from the moor — particularly the Dart. Pony trekking is also popular.

It was once possible to cross the moor only by footways such as the Abbot's Way (between Buckfast, Buckland and Tavistock abbeys) or the Mariners' Way (from Bideford to Dartmouth). Today there are still few roads across Dartmoor. Centres for exploring the moor include Ashburton, Bovey Tracey, Chagford, Ivybridge, Moretonhampstead, Okehampton and Tavistock. Plymouth is not far from the moor, which provides an outlet for many of its inhabitants all the year around.

EXMOOR

Exmoor is Devon's second National Park, shared with neighbouring Somerset. Only one third of the park is within Devon, and it is greatly overshadowed by Dartmoor. Exmoor is in the north, and the coast eastwards from Combe Martin Bay includes the picturesque Valley of Rocks near Lynmouth. Geologically Exmoor consists of Devonian sandstones and grits. The western edge rises sharply and the flatter summits and ridges have numerous prehistoric barrows and standing stones, although less well known than those on Dartmoor. The highest point is 1617 feet (493 metres) on Western Common near Kinsford Gate.

The upland has heather and grass moorland which has suffered from 'improvement' over the years. This is hill-farming country with sheep, cattle and ponies, and despite the creation of the National Park in 1954 ploughing and afforestation have continued to make inroads into the remaining moorland. As with Dartmoor this was once a royal hunting forest, but it differs in that red deer still roam the heights and are hunted by hounds. North-flowing rivers pass through attractive steep valleys where access is only by walking or riding. The lower sections are extremely steep and thickly wooded, such as at Watersmeet on the East Lyn river, Heddon's Mouth and Cleave. Exmoor was made famous by R. D.

The Torridge estuary at Appledore.

Blackmore's book *Lorna Doone*. Oare church of the book is in Somerset, but the two counties share the Doone Country as the border follows the valley of Badgworthy Water.

Lynton and Lynmouth make an important centre on the north coast, reached by the A39, which follows a tortuous course around the northern side of Exmoor. The road enters Devon at County Gate, where a fine viewpoint has been provided. The only other settlement of significance is the village of Parracombe, a few miles inland. Three minor roads from Lynmouth, Blackmoor Gate and Brayford converge on Simonsbath in Somerset and give the best access to the higher parts in the west. The B3223 from Lynmouth climbs on to one of the best parts of moorland at Brendon Common. From Kinsford Gate, a scenic road follows the lonely ridge along the Somerset border south-east for 8 miles (12.8 km) to West Anstey Common, where the Froude Hancock Stone was erected in 1935 in memory of a well known staghunter.

NORTH DEVON

A vast tract of rolling farmland and woodland lies between Exmoor and Dartmoor. Here, Barnstaple is the largest town and there are many remote villages. Much of this land lies at over 500 feet (152 metres) and rises to 764 feet (233 metres) on the more windswept Hartland peninsula. Its rocks are mainly of Carboniferous age and are a mixture of sandstones, grits, shales and slates. They are known as the Culm measures, a misleading name derived from a soft sooty 'coal' which is found only occasionally. More recent deposits of clays have been exploited around Petrockstow and at Fremington. Devonian rocks are found to the north of the Taw estuary and extend eastwards through Exmoor into Somerset. They are mainly grits and sandstones, collectively known as the Old Red Sandstone.

The north Devon coast is quite different from the south. In the very north the heights of Exmoor descend to the Bristol Channel giving tall cliffs mixed with small bays. East of Lynmouth, Foreland Point with its lighthouse is Devon's most northerly point. At Combe Martin, Lynmouth and Watermouth, where valleys descend to the shore, trading vessels were formerly beached, while Ilfracombe has a good harbour and is the only sizable town along the coast. Fishing and trade were important and there was once a busy summer traffic with Bristol Channel steamers calling at the outer pier. The coast turns abruptly south and changes to alternating headlands and bays such as Morte and Baggy Points and Woolacombe Bay. This is a classic coastline formed where alternate hard and soft rocks lie at right angles to the eroding action of the waves. Next, the double estuary of the Taw and Torridge has Saunton Sands backed by Braunton Burrows, contrasting with the pebble ridge at Westward Ho! and with Northam Burrows on the south side. West of here the coast is again north-facing and includes picturesque Clovelly. The coast turns south once more at

10

Hartland Point and fierce jagged rocks present a formidable shore and danger to shipping.

SOUTH HAMS

This is the tract of Devon which lies south of Dartmoor, between the lower Dart and Erme rivers. It means 'the land of enclosed pastures'. The rocks are mainly Devonian shales and slates. Coral limestone is found at Plymouth, Torbay and Chudleigh and has been worked for aggregates, building stone and as a 'marble' for decorative work around Ashburton and Torquay. Along the coast between Bolt Tail and Start Point is a narrow belt of schists, possibly altered Devonian or earlier rocks. The soils are well drained and support pasture and arable farming, but the landscape is dissected by deep valleys, where many of the steeper slopes are wooded. High hedges give protection from the wind, although the southern tops near the coast are windswept and treeless. The climate is mild, influenced by the sea, and sheltered parts are particular havens. However, winter blizzards can sweep across this southern part of Devon. The main settlements include Totnes, Kingsbridge and Modbury, while ports are Dartmouth and Salcombe. Farming remains important, but tourism has grown rapidly around the coastal areas.

The coast is a major attraction, indented by drowned valleys or rias as at Dartmouth and Salcombe, and with bold headlands between Bolt Head and Start Point. There are sandy beaches and small coves, such as the popular Hope Cove, and the long sweep of Slapton Sands which holds back the freshwater Ley. Burgh Island lies off Bigbury-on-Sea and is reached at high tide by a motorised sea-tractor.

Part of the South Hams was taken over and villages were evacuated during the Second World War to enable American forces to train for the D-Day landings. This centred on Slapton Sands, where during Operation Tiger in April 1944 over 30,000 troops landed, not without mishap. A monument at Torcross records the hundreds of men who died in this tragedy. The sheltered and deep-water harbours at Dartmouth and Salcombe were ideal for the gathering and equipping of vessels for the Normandy armada and much activity was seen in the months prior to June 1944.

EAST DEVON

The scenery of east Devon is much underrated. It is characterised by hills planed off to form a distinct plateau surface with steep escarpments, cut by the beautiful broad valleys of the Axe, Coly, Otter, Sid and Umborne Brook. There is a larger plateau area in the northern part around Dunkeswell, beyond which the country merges with the Blackdown

Hills in Somerset. Mainly Cretaceous greensands and grits, their poor soils support heaths and some woodland. Honiton is the main inland settlement, but Axminster and Ottery St Mary are also important. On the coast Exmouth, Sidmouth and Seaton are the principal resorts. Beer Head has the most southerly exposure of chalk in England, and there is more chalk along the coast eastwards to the Dorset border. To the south-west of Exeter an outlier of the greensand at Haldon Hill is capped with younger gravels and sand. Beyond, the Bovey basin is filled with quality clays derived from Dartmoor, and these have long been exploited in open pits and mines.

Devon's red country of rolling hills lies to the east of Dartmoor, from Tiverton down past Exeter to the coast. The New Red Sandstones of the Permian and Triassic produce the famous red soils best seen in the striking cliffs between Dawlish and Teignmouth, so well known to railway travellers. South of here the limestone cliffs and islands off Torquay provide another change.

LUNDY

Lundy, or 'puffin island', is just 3 miles (4.8 km) long and half a mile (0.8 km) wide and lies in the Bristol Channel 12 miles (19 km) north-west of Hartland Point. It is almost entirely granite, but younger than Dartmoor at 55 million years old. Only at the south-east tip are older Devonian slates. Rising to over 400 feet (122 metres), the island is prominent from the north Devon coast on clear days, as well as being a fine platform for viewing the coasts of Devon and across to South Wales, Gower and Pembrokeshire. On clear nights many lighthouses can be observed on both sides of the Channel as far away as Cornwall.

Man has occupied the island since mesolithic times, and archaeological remains include bronze age and iron age settlements. Lundy was fortified by the violent and piratical de Mariscos from the mid twelfth century and was among the last Royalist strongholds to surrender at the end of the Civil War. Farming has always been carried on, today with sheep, cattle and Lundy's own breed of pony. Grazing is shared with rabbits and sika deer. Industry came in the 1860s with an attempt to develop granite quarries on the east side. Lundy has three lighthouses; the Old Light (1820) on Beacon Hill was so often shrouded in mist that it was replaced by the North and South Lights in 1897.

Lundy is owned by the National Trust but administered by the Landmark Trust. The usual method of getting there is by the MS *Oldenburgh*, which sails from Bideford Quay and Ilfracombe. Landing is by launch to a beach. These are day trips, but there is a choice of unusual accommodation for visitors.

11

The Devil's Slide on the west coast of Lundy.

There are fewer than twenty residents in the small village, where the shop sells souvenirs and the famous Lundy puffin stamps. There is also the Marisco Tavern, a brewery and a display on Lundy's history and wildlife in the Linhay. Visitors come to Lundy for solitude, wildlife, climbing and diving. There are puffins, seals, the Lundy cabbage and much more of interest. The sea around Lundy was declared Britain's first underwater nature reserve in 1986. The finest coast is on the west side, where the Devil's Slide is a spectacular granite slab sloping into the sea. A deep hole at Shutter Point is known as the Devil's Limekiln. Montagu Steps were cut down the cliff near Great Shutter during the salvage of one of Lundy's more famous shipwrecks, the battleship HMS *Montagu*, which was wrecked during a fog in 1906.

2
Coast and country

Becky Falls, Manaton, near Bovey Tracey. Telephone: 064722 259. On the B3344, 3½ miles (5.6 km) north-west of Bovey Tracey.

There are paths and nature trails through scenic woodland where the Becka Brook tumbles among granite boulders on the edge of Dartmoor. A longer walk descends to the Teign river, where one can cross to Lustleigh village.

Beer Head and Branscombe Mouth

The chalk promontory of Beer Head is a short walk south from Beer village. Great towers of chalk rise from an overgrown landslip below the main head. To the west the steep chalk gives way to sloping cliffs of red sandstone behind a long shingle beach. The easiest access is at Branscombe Mouth and for 3 miles (4.8 km) the cliffs continue to Dunscombe Cliff, broken again only at Weston Mouth. Much of this is National Trust property and can also be approached from Sidmouth.

Belstone Common, Belstone. The village lies 2 miles (3.2 km) south-east of Okehampton.

A good introduction to the north part of Dartmoor, this is approached from Belstone village. The boulder-strewn Belstone Tor rises to 1567 feet (478 metres) between the East Okement and Taw rivers, the latter starting at Taw Marsh. The Ninestones at the foot of the tor is a retaining stone circle for a burial mound. Across the south end of the hill is the Irishman's Wall, said to have been built by

Irishmen but breached by the locals, who feared enclosure of the moor.

Berry Head Country Park, Brixham.

This headland of Devonian limestone at the south end of Torbay has rare plants, such as the white rock-rose, and a colony of sea birds on the cliffs, notably guillemots and kittiwakes. The north part of the headland was extensively quarried over 150 years until 1969, when the country park was created. There are substantial remains of Napoleonic-period fortifications (see chapter 4), while the lighthouse seems small because height is unnecessary as the headland is 200 feet (61 metres) above sea level. Views are superb, across the whole of Torbay and sometimes along the Devon and Dorset coast as far as Portland. Offshore heavily laden supertankers may be seen discharging oil into smaller vessels to enable them to enter the shallow waters of north European ports. To the south-west is Sharkham Point, where iron ore was once quarried.

Blackingstone Rock, near Moretonhampstead.

Also aptly called the Pudding Stone, this is a most curious upstanding granite tor on a hill 2 miles (3.2 km) east of Moretonhampstead. Closely spaced joints follow the shape of the hillside down a long north face. Steep stone steps on the east side allow access to the summit. Heltor Rock is a similar rock 1¼ miles (2 km) to the north-east.

Bolt Head to Bolt Tail. National Trust.

There is an exhilarating 6 mile (9.6 km) cliff walk along south Devon's most wild and rugged coast westwards from Overbecks at Salcombe harbour entrance to Hope Cove. The jagged rocks are an ancient schist also found at Start Point. The beautiful Finnish barque *Herzogin Cecile* came to grief on this coast in 1936, when she struck the Ham Stone off Soar Mill Cove. Laden with grain, this four-master was refloated and beached in Starehole Bay, where she broke up.

Braunton Burrows nature reserve, 2 miles (3.2 km) west of Braunton.

A strange dune landscape, grassy and mountainous, with a great expanse of Saunton Sands exposed at low tide, the Burrows are very extensive and an important nature reserve on the north side of the Taw-Torridge estuary.

Buckland Beacon. Near a lane on to the moor 2½ miles (4 km) north-west of Ashburton.

An exceptional viewpoint at 1281 feet (390 metres), this looks out over the Dart gorge from the moorland edge. Of added interest are two granite slabs, one at an angle, carved with the Ten Commandments in 1928. An inscription on the summit recalls a bonfire lit to celebrate the silver jubilee of George V. One mile (1.6 km) west is Buckland-in-the-Moor, where the church clock face has its numerals replaced by the words MY DEAR MOTHER.

Burrator Reservoir, Sheepstor, near Yelverton.

This beautiful lake was created to provide Plymouth's main water supply by the construction of a granite dam in 1898, which was heightened in 1928. Today the reservoir of 150 acres (61 ha) is in a most attractive setting surrounded by conifers and some oakwood, with moorland hills such as the craggy Leather Tor and Sheeps Tor rising behind. A scenic road surrounds the whole lake. The Devonport Leat of 1793 can be seen on the west side. Not far from the dam are the church villages of Meavy and Sheepstor.

Canonteign Falls and Country Park, Canonteign, Lower Ashton, near Chudleigh. Telephone: 0647 52666.

A tributary on the west bank of the Teign provides the setting for a gorge landscaped by the first Viscountess Exmouth, who also built Canonteign House. Long overgrown, this was revealed again in 1985. The Lady Exmouth Falls cascade for 220 feet (67 metres) and are the highest in England. Other features include the Clampitt Falls, Devil's Leap, ornamental lakes, a panoramic viewpoint and picnic areas.

Combe Martin Bay, Combe Martin.

There is superb coastal scenery from the narrow inlet of Water Mouth in the west to the tall cliffs of the Little Hangman and Great Hangman, 1043 feet (318 metres) high, in the east, accessible by the A399 and coastal footpath at Combe Martin.

Dartmeet, Dartmoor.

The boulder-strewn East and West Dart rivers meet here before the enlarged river continues for many miles through wooded gorge scenery to New Bridge and Holne Bridge. These carry the same Ashburton to Tavistock B3357 road which crosses the East Dart at Dartmeet by a stone arched bridge. A ruined clapper bridge is just upstream. The picturesque Huccaby Bridge across the West Dart is nearby on the lane to Hexworthy.

Dawlish Warren nature reserve, Dawlish Warren.

A spit of over a mile (1.6 km) almost blocks the entrance to the Exe estuary opposite Exmouth. Behind the beach there are sand dunes and a nature reserve. Among the rare plants, the Jersey lily has its only habitat in mainland England. A small ferry crosses to and from Exmouth.

Dewerstone Rocks, near Shaugh Prior, Plymouth. National Trust.

Granite crags rise dramatically above the oak woodland on the valleyside of the Plym just upstream from its confluence with the Meavy at Shaugh Bridge. The main Devil's Rock provides hard rock climbs of nearly 200 feet (61 metres). Upper crags include the Needle and Raven Buttresses. In the same woodland are the remains of old quarries and a tramway system with an incline, while on the spur above is an iron age promontory fort.

Dowlands Cliffs and Landslips nature reserve, near Axmouth.

The coast from Axmouth to the Dorset border at Lyme Regis suffered a huge landslip in 1839. This has remained undisturbed by man, so its atmosphere, wildlife and geology are unsurpassed.

Fernworthy Forest and Reservoir, near Chagford.

Lanes from Chagford or Moretonhampstead give access to the five-fingered Fernworthy Reservoir near the head of the South Teign river. The dam was completed in 1942 to provide water for Torquay, but much of the extensive forest in the catchment area was planted earlier. Under the conifers are hut-circles, stone rows and a circle.

Fingle Bridge, near Drewsteignton.

This sixteenth-century packhorse bridge crosses the Teign amidst the scenic wooded Teign valley, which has gorge-like proportions. Prestonbury Castle hillfort overlooks the bridge from a spur to the east (see chapter 3). There is a good walk up the valley to Castle Drogo (see chapter 6), while a much longer walk of 4½ miles (7.2 km) follows the river downstream almost entirely through woodland past Clifford Bridge to Steps Bridge, another popular spot and nature reserve near Dunsford.

Glen Lyn Gorge, Lynmouth.

The West Lyn river falls steeply down a ravine near the bottom of Lynmouth Hill. Much was swept away in the 1952 flood, but restoration has continued since 1961 so that now footpaths wind up through woods past cascades and waterfalls to the ravine. A hydro-electric power plant was opened in September 1985, the largest private scheme in England. The Exhibition Hall in an old chapel near the entrance covers many aspects of water power and includes steam locomotive models and photographs of the 1952 Lyn floods and the difficult construction of the hydro-electric scheme.

Great Staple Tor, near Merrivale.

Tall pillars of granite blocks make up this impressive tor, which is reached by easy walking from the B3357 road 4 miles (6.4 km) from Tavistock, and close to Merrivale with its working granite quarry. At 1493 feet (455 metres) and almost at the edge of Dartmoor, there are wide views westward to the Cornish hills and south-west to Plymouth. Across Whitchurch Common to the south of the road is the sphinx-like form of Vixen Tor. Pew Tor has good rocks further south and is accessible

Fingle Bridge over the Teign near Drewsteignton.

Haytor Rocks on Dartmoor.

from Tavistock.

Haldon Hill, near Chudleigh.

This forested upland rises to over 750 feet (228 metres) south of Exeter and presents a barrier crossed by the busy A38 and A380 roads, the former at Great Haldon, where there is a racecourse on the summit. To the north-west are forested walks and a viewpoint at the prominent Lawrence Castle. A spiral staircase to the top of this three-sided folly gives breathtaking views over Exeter and the Exe and Teign valleys. A ridge continues to the south, ending at Little Haldon with viewpoints above Teignmouth.

Hallsands, Start Bay. 2 miles (3.2 km) south of Torcross on Slapton Sands.

Here are the ruins of a fishing village almost entirely swept away during a gale in 1917. This was not a total surprise, as the protecting shingle bank had been severely eroded due to the offshore dredging of thousands of tons of gravel used in the Devonport Dockyard extensions at the end of the nineteenth century.

Hartland Point and Quay

There is a lighthouse down on the point at this north-west corner of Devon. Southwards past Damehole Point, Hartland Quay and Speke's Mill Mouth to the Cornish border at Marsland Mouth the coast is fearsome, with jagged strata at right angles to the shore, a grave for any ship unlucky enough to run aground. The wreck of the fleet tanker *Green Ranger* in 1962 is still remembered but others since include the coaster *Johanna* twenty years later. At Speke's Mill Mouth a 70 foot (21 metre) waterfall descends to the shore. Hartland Quay was built by the monks of Hartland

Abbey, improved in the sixteenth century and washed away in 1896. Today there are a small slipway, a hotel and museum (see chapter 7).

Haytor Rocks, accessible from the Widecombe road 4 miles (6.4 km) west of Bovey Tracey.

This is one of the great viewpoints of Dartmoor, with outstanding views southwards to the sea. A rounded pillowy mass of granite forms the main tor, behind which is Low Man, insignificant on the south side but with a 100 foot (30 metre) face on the north. The Haytor quarries and granite tramway are important relics here (see chapter 8).

Heddon's Mouth and Cleave, near Martinhoe.

The Cleave is a steep defile about 650 feet (200 metres) deep which descends to Heddon's Mouth on the north Devon coast between Combe Martin and Lynton. From the Hunter's Inn, where the valley is wooded, there are paths on both sides of the stream for a mile (1.6 km) to the shore, where there is an old limekiln.

High Willhays and Yes Tor, near Okehampton.

South of Okehampton are the highest Dartmoor summits, rising to 2038 feet (621 metres) and 2030 feet (619 metres) respectively. A keen walker could start from Meldon Reservoir and include the West Okement valley with its ancient oak woodland of Black Tor Beare in a rewarding circular tour.

Hound Tor, 2 miles (3.2 km) north-east of Widecombe.

A classic Dartmoor tor, showing how weathering has exploited the tabular nature of the jointing within the granite to reveal towers like

Bowerman's Nose, near Hound Tor.

building blocks separated by wide avenues. Just to the south-east an excavated medieval village is worth a visit (see chapter 3), while the readily recognised forms of Haytor and Low Man stand out on the horizon beyond. A lane to the north from Hound Tor leads towards Bowerman's Nose, an upstanding chimney of granite on the north side of Hayne Down.

Lydford Gorge, Lydford, Okehampton. National Trust.

This ranks among the most attractive river walks in Britain. At the start near Lydford village the young river Lyd crashes through a water-smoothed ravine carved from the rock with potholes. A walkway gives access to the Devil's Cauldron, although for safety reasons it is closed in winter or when the river is in spate. Less wild but highly attractive is the walk of 2 miles (3.2 km) through mature woodland following the gorge of the Lyd. At the end is the White Lady, a slender 90 foot (27 metre) cascade into a pool on the south side.

Morte Bay, Woolacombe. National Trust.

2 miles (3.2 km) of sandy beach are enclosed by the fine headlands of Morte Point and Baggy Point. To the north is Bull Point with a lighthouse, and to the south the smaller Croyde Bay. Despite development around Woolacombe and Croyde, much of the coastline is protected by the National Trust.

Northam Burrows Country Park, Northam.

Over 600 acres (243 ha) of grassy dunes and saltmarsh lie behind the pebble ridge at Westward Ho! on the south side of the entrance to the Taw-Torridge estuary. Nature trails are provided.

North Devon Coast Path

The Devon border 12 miles (19.2 km) west of Minehead is the start of the 550 mile (880 km) South West Way to Poole Harbour. The high cliffs along the north coast of Exmoor change to west-facing headlands and fine sandy bays at Morte and Croyde. After Saunton Sands and Braunton Burrows the coast is broken by the Taw-Torridge estuary, where the final section of the coast path was opened in 1987. Beyond the shingle bank at Westward Ho! the coast continues past Buck's Mills and Clovelly to the dramatic cliffs and jagged rocks of Hartland Point and Quay. The path joins the Cornish section at lonely Marsland Mouth.

Plym Bridge Woods, near Plymouth. National Trust.

There are woodland walks just north-east of Plymouth, mostly between the thirteenth-century Plym Bridge and the Cann Viaduct of the former Tavistock branch railway. Slate was extracted near the viaduct at a quarry which was once served by a canal and tramway (see chapter 8).

Postbridge, Dartmoor.

This is the best known clapper bridge on Dartmoor, being next to the B3212 road from Moretonhampstead. Stone piers support great slabs of granite forming a footway, originally for packhorses rather than wheeled traffic. Probably medieval, Postbridge was reconstructed in 1880 when one stone was replaced after being thrown down about 55 years earlier to form a duck pool in the East Dart river. Just downstream at Bellever there is an attractive three-arched bridge beside a broken clapper bridge. There are also forest walks and access to the moor.

Prawle Point. National Trust.

This is the most southerly part of Devon, with a coastguard lookout. It is best approached from the village of East Prawle, and there is good walking west to Salcombe harbour and east to Lannacombe Beach and Start Point.

River Dart Country Park, Holne Park, Ashburton. Telephone: 0364 52511.

Nature trails, a tree trail, adventure playgrounds, woodland and riverside walks are all part of this park beside the river Dart just west of Ashburton. The house is a residential centre and there are also camping and caravanning facilities in the grounds.

Slapton Sands and Ley. The A379 Kingsbridge to Dartmouth road runs along the beach.

A 2¼ mile (3.6 km) sand and shingle bank

Above: *The White Lady waterfall in Lydford Gorge.*

Below: *The clapper bridge and three-arched bridge at Bellever, near Postbridge.*

holds back the freshwater Slapton Ley, a nature reserve served by a field centre in Slapton village. The beach was used by the United States forces to practise the Normandy Landings in 1944, and there are memorials beside the road at the north end of the Ley and at Torcross. The latter includes a Sherman tank salvaged from the sea and a memorial erected in 1987 to the dead of the ill-fated Operation Tiger.

South Devon Coast Path

This section is 93 miles (149 km) from Plymouth to Lyme Regis, just across the border in Dorset. The coast is less harsh than the north but varies considerably, with seven major estuaries (all but one crossed by ferry), the cliffs of the wild Bolt Head and Tail, the great sweep of Slapton Sands and the softer red sandstone and white chalk cliffs of east Devon. All this contrasts with the major urbanised section from Torbay to Dawlish.

Start Point, 6 miles (9.6 km) east of Salcombe.

A narrow neck of ancient schists protrudes into the sea at the south end of Start Bay. The cliffs are not high, but the lighthouse gives added interest. To the west is the tiny Lannacombe Beach, and between there are good examples of raised beaches — grassy terraces indicating former shorelines.

Stover Country Park, near Newton Abbot.

This landscaped park with woodland around a lake, close to the junction of the A38 and A382 north-west of Newton Abbot, was once the grounds of Stover House, the home of the Templers, who developed the Stover Canal and Haytor Tramway (see chapter 8). The Templer Way passes the park as it follows the canal and tramway from Haytor to the Teign estuary.

Two Moors Way, Ivybridge to Lynmouth.

This long-distance footpath of 102 miles (163 km) from Ivybridge to Lynmouth, taking in parts of both Dartmoor and Exmoor, was opened in 1976. A section near Gidleigh on Dartmoor incorporates the much older Mariners' Way, once used by sailors walking between the ports of Dartmouth and Bideford.

Valley of Rocks, Lynton.

This famous dry valley was probably a glacial meltwater channel formed when ice touched the north Devon coast during the ice age. It is separated from the coast by rocky tors such as Lion Rock. A hole under a leaning slab is called the White Lady as its outline resembles a lady in period costume. On the seaward side is a splendid path cut from Lynmouth in 1830. At the west end are Lee Bay and Lee Abbey, a Christian community

centre. The road continues to Woody Bay, where it is surprising to find houses far down the steep wooded cliffs.

Watersmeet. Beside the A39, 1½ miles (2.4 km) upstream from Lynmouth. National Trust.

This is a popular location, with attractive walks from the meeting of the steep wooded valleys of the East Lyn and Hoaroak Water. Watersmeet House is a fishing lodge of about 1832, now serving for information, refreshments and a shop.

Wembury Bay and Yealm estuary. National Trust.

There is good coastal scenery on both shores at the mouth of the Yealm estuary. On the north side is Wembury with its cliff-top church and an old mill by the beach which is now a cafe. To the west is HMS *Cambridge*, a Royal Navy gunnery range, while offshore is the pyramidal Great Mew Stone, whose last residents in the 1830s were the part-time smuggler Sam Wakeham and his family. The cliffs on the south side can be approached from Newton Ferrers and Noss Mayo and the path follows part of the Nine Mile Drive laid out in the nineteenth century by Lord Revelstoke of nearby Membland Hall.

Wistman's Wood nature reserve, near Two Bridges, Dartmoor.

A woodland of ancient stunted oaks cloaked in mosses, lichens and ferns survives amongst granite boulders on the east side of the West Dart valley one mile (1.6 km) north of Two Bridges. It may be a remnant of the original forest cover on Dartmoor, as may Black Tor Beare and Piles Copse. Across the valley is the start of the Devonport Leat.

Woodbury Common, near Woodbury. The viewpoint is on the B3180, 4 miles (6.4 km) inland from Exmouth.

The high ground north of Exmouth has extensive heathland and some pine woods. A viewpoint at 564 feet (172 metres) looks out over the Exe estuary with Dartmoor beyond, and along the south Devon coast. Woodbury Castle is a hillfort (see chapter 3). The extensive heath includes Colaton Raleigh Common, while Aylesbeare Common to the north is a nature reserve.

Yarner Wood National Nature Reserve, near Bovey Tracey.

This mainly oak wood of 375 acres (150 ha) lies below the moorland of Haytor Down 2 miles (3.2 km) west of Bovey Tracey. There are nature trails although access to a large portion of the wood is by permit only.

Spinsters' Rock is Devon's best surviving chambered tomb.

3
Places of archaeological interest

Evidence for palaeolithic man comes from cave sites near the south Devon coast, such as Ash Hole and Windmill caverns at Brixham and the world-famous Kents Cavern at Torquay. Hand axes have been recovered from river gravels near Axminster. The first field monuments appeared in the neolithic, but unlike Cornwall, where chambered tombs are relatively common, the Spinsters' Rock is the only convincing example in Devon. Another is at Corringdon Ball, while a less well known one is at Broadsands near Paignton. Devon has some notable settlements. The well known iron age hillfort at Hembury overlies a causewayed enclosure, with a much earlier date of around 4000 BC. Elsewhere, the post holes of a rectangular house have been excavated on Haldon Hill. Other likely settlement sites include High Peak at Sidmouth and Hazard Hill west of Totnes.

Dartmoor presents one of Britain's finest outdoor archaeological museums of the bronze age, with its numerous stone circles, stone rows, standing stones and villages of hut-circles and field systems. The wealth of Dartmoor greatly overshadows the rest of the county, where the principal iron age and later monuments are found. Many sites are at a high level, inhospitable in twentieth-century climate but evidence of drier and warmer conditions in the past. The inhabitants were mainly

pastoral, although some fields were cultivated. Poor acid soils and altitude have always made Dartmoor a marginal farming area and climatic deterioration led to sites being abandoned in favour of lower levels in the middle and late bronze age. Being made of moorland granite much has survived and the prehistoric landscape is almost perfectly preserved. One finds hut villages, some within great stone-walled pounds as at Grimspound, fields and 'reaves' related to boundaries of farming communities such as on Holne Moor. Dartmoor is also renowned for its ritual monuments: stone circles, standing stones and stone rows, some very long. There are burial cairns too, and coffin-like stone cists.

Exmoor's high crests also have barrows, stone circles and stone rows. Little suitable stone was available elsewhere in Devon, but there are barrow groups on higher ground, such as Woodbury Common and Broad Down in the south-east, and Bursdon Moor and Berry Down in the north.

Although some parts of Dartmoor such as Kestor were not abandoned, the principal iron age and later monuments are found elsewhere in the county. Iron age hillforts are mostly in the south and east of the county, where Hembury has been described by the landscape historian W. G. Hoskins as the 'grandest earthwork in Devon'. Unusual forts include

19

Clovelly Dykes with its widely spaced ramparts interpreted as cattle pounds, a type also seen at Prestonbury Castle and at Milber near Newton Abbot. At the latter small bronze animals were found during excavations. Cliff castles are more characteristic of the coasts of Cornwall, Pembrokeshire (Dyfed) and Brittany, but there is a good example at Bolt Tail. Another at Berry Head is now lost beneath later defences (see chapter 4). Others at High Peak and Branscombe in east Devon are more akin to hillforts. At least two trading ports have been recognised, at Mount Batten and Topsham, with evidence of contact with Gaul and probably the Mediterranean world. The iron age people of Devon and Cornwall were known as the Dumnonii, who used no coins but traded by barter. So-called iron currency bars have been found near the fort at Holne Chase.

Within a few years of the Roman invasion, the Fosse Way was built from Lincoln to the Devon coast at Axmouth, later branching to Exeter (*Isca Dumnoniorum*), along the line now followed by the A30 from Honiton. Exeter became the only major Roman centre in Devon, with a fortress and walled town. Excavations have revealed parts of Roman Exeter, in particular the legionary bath-house. Sections of the town wall survive, much patched in later years. Topsham was a port, although shipping could reach *Isca*. From Exeter, a road led south-west towards Totnes, itself a probable Roman site. A second road continued westwards from Exeter to Cornwall. The earthworks of a posting station survive close to the railway near North Tawton, where there is a Roman pillar in the churchyard. Further along the way a small fort has been discovered just north of Okehampton. Earthworks overlooking the Bristol Channel at Martinhoe and Old Burrow were military signal stations, while a third was on Stoke Hill just outside Exeter. Villas are rare in Devon and confined to the south-east, where at least two are known.

Apart from many place-names, the Saxons left little physical evidence. There are earthworks of the old Saxon *burh* at Lydford (see chapter 4) and a fine carved cross at Copplestone which may date from the tenth century. The Braunton Great Field in north Devon may be of Saxon origin, although it was not recorded until the early fourteenth century. It covers 350 acres (140 ha) but its seven hundred strips have been greatly reduced in number by amalgamation over the years. Castles of the medieval period are described in chapter 4, but the village of long houses at Hound Tor shows that the fringes of Dartmoor were recolonised for farming when the climate ameliorated. The best of the strip lynchets which occur on Dartmoor are at Challacombe

Down and are visible from Grimspound. Farming on Dartmoor was often related to tin streaming, for it was necessary to combine occupations to gain a meagre living.

Archaeological finds are held by many local museums, but especially Exeter's Royal Albert Memorial Museum (see chapter 7). The following sites have been selected for their importance and ease of access. In the case of Dartmoor, anyone prepared to walk further will be rewarded by much more. The name of each site is followed by the Ordnance Survey 1:50,000 map sheet on which it appears, together with the six-figure grid reference.

Blackbury Castle hillfort, Southleigh (OS 192: SY 187924). 1½ miles (2.4 km) south-west of Southleigh near Colyton.

This small iron age hillfort lies along a ridge. The entrance on the south side has complex outer defences, probably unfinished.

Bolt Tail cliff castle, Hope (OS 202: SX 670397). Footpath from Hope Cove.

A rampart up to 15 feet (4.6 metres) high crosses the neck of this superb promontory, creating an iron age fort which commands Bigbury Bay and the subsidiary Hope Cove.

Butterdon stone row, Harford (OS 202: SX 656588 to SX 654607). Walk from Ivybridge or Harford.

There are several cairns on Butterdon Hill. A double line of small stones begins at one low cairn with a fallen retaining circle. It leads north for 1¼ miles (2 km) to the summit of Piles Hill, where it ends at a fallen standing stone. There are other bronze age stone rows and cairns here.

Cadbury Castle hillfort, Cadbury (OS 192: SS 914053). Approach from Fursdon House (see chapter 6).

This iron age hillfort is univallate, with the highest section of rampart on the south side. Within, a 54 foot (16.4 metre) ritual shaft was excavated in the mid nineteenth century and was found to contain votive offerings of bronze bracelets, rings, beads, pottery and bones of late Roman date. The fort is on the highest point and provides excellent views.

Capton prehistoric site, Dittisham (OS 202: SX 839536).

This is a hilltop in the South Hams recently found to have had a long history of occupation. A small museum has finds of all periods from the palaeolithic to medieval times, and a reconstructed neolithic house helps explain the archaeology. A much ruined chambered tomb has been found on the hilltop, from which some remarkable alignments have been measured, suggesting the site may have had great significance.

Chapman Barrows, Challacombe (OS 180: SS 695435). At the west end of The Chains between Challacombe and Parracombe parishes.

This is a superb site for a bronze age cemetery. Eleven barrows at over 1500 feet (457 metres) look out over the Bristol Channel and inland to Dartmoor. Just south-east along the ridge are the 9 foot (2.7 metre) Longstone, Exmoor's tallest standing stone, and Longstone Barrow.

Clovelly Dykes hillfort, Clovelly (OS 190: SS 311235). At the junction of the B3237 to Clovelly with the A39.

This substantial iron age hillfort is best viewed from the air. The main fort has two rectilinear enclosures and is surrounded by three outer ramparts, especially well developed on the west side. The enclosures created by these widely spaced earthworks may have been stock pounds for protection or for the autumn gathering and slaughter.

Corringdon Ball long barrow,, South Brent (OS 202: SX 670614).

This is a rare example of a neolithic chambered long barrow on Dartmoor. The ruined chamber is at the south-east end of a mound 141 feet (43 metres) long. When seen from the west, the barrow is prominent on the skyline of the saddle between the Avon and Glaze Brook. There are bronze age stone rows just to the west.

Countisbury promontory fort, Lynmouth (OS 180: SS 141493). On the A39 between Lynmouth and Countisbury.

A great rampart at Wind Hill cuts off the promontory where the Lyn valley lies parallel to the coast before entering the sea. It is well defended on all other sides by the steep valley and the sea cliffs. The size of the enclosed area suggests this may have been an invasion beach-head of the iron age. The A39 coast road passes through the site.

Cranbrook Castle hillfort, Moretonhampstead (OS 191: SX 738890).

An almost square hillfort enclosing 8 acres (3.2 ha) has a single stone-faced rampart, smaller on the north side, which overlooks the very steep Teign gorge. Opposite is Prestonbury, another iron age fort.

Dumpdon Great Camp hillfort, Luppitt (OS 192: ST 176040). National Trust.

A clump of trees on Dumpdon Hill makes this a prominent landmark, best seen from the A303 near Honiton. The iron age fort has an inturned entrance on the north-east side.

Exeter Roman town (OS 192: SX 919927).

A small fort was established at Exeter shortly after the Roman invasion, but the Roman town of *Isca Dumnoniorum* was not laid out on the north-west until after AD 75. A hundred years later its 92 acres (37 ha) were enclosed by a ditch and rampart, and a wall was added using local stone soon after AD 200. This later became the medieval town wall, but parts of the Roman structure can still be seen. The four medieval gateways which replaced the Roman ones were demolished in the early nineteenth century. Excavations have revealed some of the pattern of Roman Exeter, but the most spectacular find was the legionary bath-house in the Cathedral Close. Many small finds are in the Royal Albert Memorial Museum (see chapter 7).

Farway Hill barrows, near Honiton (OS 192: SY 159958). At the centre of over fifty barrows on the narrow plateau south of Honiton, between Gittisham Hill (SY 148963) and Broad Down (SY 170937), and mostly visible from the B3174.

Excavations have shown these to be of beaker and early bronze age date, with evidence of complex rituals at some sites. A handled shale cup was found in one barrow at Broad Down.

Five Barrows, near Brayford (OS 180: SS 734368). Access is from a lane on the Somerset border, half a mile (0.8 km) from Kinsford Gate.

Despite the name, there are at least eight bronze age barrows here on Western Common, high up on the south-western edge of Exmoor at 1617 feet (493 metres). The Setta Barrow (SS 726381) is one mile (1.6 km) north-west and has a well preserved peristalith, or circle of retaining stones.

Foales Arishes settlement, near Widecombe (OS 191: SX 737758).

Eight hut-circles were excavated in 1896, but only six are now visible. The period of occupation includes the late bronze age and early iron age. Associated field systems have been covered by medieval strip fields and the whole site was later altered by nineteenth-century agriculture.

Grey Wethers stone circles, Dartmoor (OS 191: SX 639831). Approach from the Fernworthy forest and reservoir or, further but more interesting, up the East Dart valley from Postbridge.

Here at 1400 feet (427 metres) are a remote pair of restored bronze age circles, the only ones on Dartmoor.

Excavated longhouses at the Hound Tor medieval village, Dartmoor.

Grimspound enclosed settlement, Manaton (OS 191: SX 701809).

This is the best known of its type on Dartmoor and lies at 1500 feet (457 metres). A thick stone wall surrounds an area of about 4 acres (1.6 ha), with a strongly built entrance on the south side. Enclosures built against the wall may have been for stock, as the inhabitants were bronze age pastoralists. There are 24 hut-circles here, some reconstructed. One shows the outer porch often found at hut-circles, built to shelter the doorway. The site slopes down to include a small stream which flows through the enclosure.

Hameldown Barrow, Widecombe (OS 191: SX 707792). On the high ridge of Hamel Down to the south of Grimspound.

This early bronze age barrow is one of the Two Barrows. It was constructed of peaty turf with a central cairn and outer cairn ring. A rich cremation burial under a slab pavement contained a grooved dagger with an amber pommel decorated with gold pins. This was unfortunately destroyed during the Second World War. The Broad Barrow and Single Barrow along the same ridge are of similar construction.

Hembury hillfort, Payhembury (OS 192: ST 113030). On a spur which slopes down to the A373 Honiton to Cullompton road.

This multivallate hillfort covers 7 acres (2.8 ha). Two great banks later reduced the size of the fort. It was occupied in the iron age down to about AD 65-70. The fort overlies a neolithic causewayed enclosure, formed by a line of discontinuous ditches and a bank which cut off the end of the spur. Within, the post holes of a gateway and rectangular house were found during excavations. Distinctive round-based pottery has been given the name Hembury ware, and grain impressions indicate a mixed farming economy. The date of this neolithic site may be as early as 4210 BC.

Hound Tor medieval village, Manaton (OS 191: SX 746788). Just downslope to the south-east of Hound Tor (see chapter 2).

Excavated walls of a settlement date from the thirteenth century when the moor was recolonised by farmers for a short time. Longhouses are clearly displayed, in which the living quarters and animal byres were all under one roof but separated by a cross passage. Other structures include three small barns with corn-drying kilns. There are also traces of trackways and field enclosures on the moor.

Kents Cavern, Wellswood, Torquay (OS 202: SX 934642).

The cavern is a show cave (see chapter 9) but the discovery of animal and human bones, with tools of antler, bone and flint, dating back 100,000 years have made this an important palaeolithic site. The main finds are in the

Torquay Museum (see chapter 7) and the Natural History Museum in London.

Kestor settlement, Chagford (OS 191: SX 665867). A lane from Teigncombe leads out on to Dartmoor and through this site.

On the right-hand (lower) side of the lane is the Round Pound, where a wall surrounds a large circular hut 37 feet (11.3 metres) in diameter, shown by excavation to have been an ironworker's hut. Features included a furnace and a drain. Other huts and rectangular iron age fields can be seen on the slopes above towards the Kestor rocks, which make a good viewing point.

Martinhoe fortlet, Martinhoe (OS 180: SS 663493).

This is a small but well defended early Roman fortlet on the cliff edge of Devon's north coast. Built as a signal station and point for observing hostile activities of the Silures across the water in South Wales, it was occupied for about fifteen years until AD 75, when the legionary fort was built at Caerleon. The double ramparts and ditches had alternate landward and seaward entrances to impede attacks. Inside were two wooden barracks for eighty men (a century), field ovens and a furnace. Excavations revealed traces of signal fires in the outer enclosure.

Merrivale prehistoric sites, Merrivale (OS 201: SX 555748). On the B3357 between Princetown and Merrivale Bridge.

The edge of this excellent bronze age site is cut by the B3357. There is a village of hut-circles on both sides of the road, although those on the south are the easiest to view. On

the open moor beyond are two parallel double stone rows aligned east-west. The longer is the south row, which has a barrow with retaining circle almost at the centre. There are cists and cairns, and from one of the latter a third row, single and rather faint, leads south-west. The ritual site also includes a small stone circle and a standing stone about 10 feet (3 metres) tall.

Old Burrow fortlet, Countisbury (OS 180: SS 788493). 2½ miles (4 km) east of Countisbury.

This small Roman fort was of a similar plan and function to Martinhoe but was earlier and occupied only in about AD 48-52. It overlooks the Bristol Channel from a site on high ground close to the Somerset border.

Plym valley prehistoric sites, Sheepstor (OS 202: SX 592670 and SX 570653). Drizzlecombe: approach by a lane from Sheepstor. Other sites: by path from Cadover Bridge.

There is much bronze age archaeology here on the north bank of the Plym. Drizzlecombe (SX 592670) has cairns with stone rows ending at standing stones, the tallest being 14 feet (4.3 metres). There are hut-circles and pounds all about, the best being further downstream at Legis Tor (SX 570653), where a pound is made up of four enclosures with hut-circles within. At Trowlesworthy Warren across the river there are more huts, pounds and stone rows on the west side of Trowlesworthy Tor (SX 574645). Amongst evidence for nineteenth-century stone-cutting between the twin Trowlesworthy tors there is an unfinished drum-shaped block of pink granite, said to have been intended for the base of a monument at Devonport.

A bronze age hut-circle at Merrivale, Dartmoor.

Prestonbury Castle hillfort, Drewsteignton (OS 191: SX 746900).

Overlooking Fingle Bridge from the north side of the Teign gorge, the main defences of this iron age hillfort are on the gentler north-east slopes. An outer rampart forms a large enclosure, perhaps for a stock pound as at Clovelly Dykes. Cranbrook Castle is another hillfort, across the gorge to the south-west.

Riders Rings enclosures, near South Brent (OS 202: SX 679644). About one mile (1.6 km) north of Shipley Bridge car park.

A double bronze age enclosure lies high up the side of the Avon valley. The south-west enclosure has sixteen huts, many against the north wall. The other pound is elongated and appears to have been added later. It has at least twelve huts, and rectangular enclosures built against the wall. These were probably for stock, although some may have been cultivation plots.

Scorhill stone circle, Gidleigh (OS 191: SX 655874).

This is one of Dartmoor's best bronze age stone circles, easily reached from Gidleigh, yet in a wild open setting. The circle of 88 feet (26.8 metres) diameter has 23 pointed stones standing and seven fallen. Many more have been removed, and several were taken to line the bank of a nearby leat.

Shoulsbury Castle hillfort, near Challacombe (OS 180: SS 706391).

This iron age hillfort encloses about 5 acres (2 ha) at the end of a hill on western Exmoor. An outer rampart and ditch on the south side may be incomplete. It was once thought to have been Roman because of its rectangular plan and the finding of two swords nearby, but these have since been dated to the seventeenth century. Shoulsbury may have been a cattle pound.

Shovel Down stone rows, Batworthy, near Chagford (OS 191: SX 659860). South-west of Kestor.

There are at least three bronze age stone rows with different alignments on this sloping site. They are double rows and one converges on a cairn of four concentric circles of stones. A second row appears to be aligned with the Scorhill circle, one mile (1.6 km) away to the north. The third climbs southwards and ends at a small cairn covering a broken cist. Just south over the ridge top are two more stone rows, one ending at the Longstone, a 10½ foot (3.2 metre) standing stone which forms the boundary of Chagford, Gidleigh and Lydford parishes.

Spinsters' Rock, Drewsteignton (OS 191: SX 701908).

This is Devon's best example of a neolithic chambered tomb. A 16 ton capstone is supported by only three tall uprights, the result of a restoration in 1862 following the collapse of the tomb earlier that year. All traces of a mound have disappeared. Tradition has it that three spinsters erected the monument one morning before breakfast.

Stall Moor stone row, Erme valley (OS 202: SX 635644 to SX 636678).

This is the longest bronze age stone row on Dartmoor, 2.1 miles (3.4 km) northwards from a small stone circle on Stall Moor to a cairn on Green Hill. It is mostly on the west side of the Erme valley but crosses the river and a tributary, disappearing beneath the peat from time to time. Both sides of the Erme valley to the north of Harford are rich in archaeological remains.

Woodbury Castle hillfort, near Woodbury (OS 192: SY 033874). On the B3180 4 miles (6.4 km) inland from Exmouth.

There are massive ramparts beneath a beech wood, cut through by the B3180. Excavations have shown that there was a hut settlement with a palisade before this iron age fort was built.

Berry Pomeroy Castle.

4
Castles and coastal fortifications

Devon has some striking castles but none is on a grand scale. There are also motte and bailey earthworks built by the barons at the time of the Norman conquest. These include **Bampton**, on a spur on the north side of the town, and **Holwell Castle**, across the stream immediately south of Parracombe church. **Heywood Wood** is on a wooded spur overlooking the Taw river, a mile (1.6 km) south-west of Chulmleigh, while at nearby **Winkleigh** there are two mounds, off Castle Street and at Court Castle. **Burley Wood** has two motte and bailey works associated with an earlier iron age fort 2 miles (3.2 km) north-west of Lydford. This interesting site is remote and difficult to see, as is **Durpley Castle**, 2 miles (3.2 km) north-west of Shebbear. In the South Hams a motte and bailey 2¾ miles (4.4 km) north of Loddiswell made use of an earlier iron age fort, called **The Rings**. Some so-called castles such as Compton and Powderham were fortified houses of the fourteenth century and they and the much altered Bickleigh Castle are described in chapter 6.

There was a need for defence around the natural harbours of the south coast, a tradition carried down from the fourteenth century into the twentieth. The chief danger was from raids by the French. Dartmouth has the first castle in England to be built for artillery, while the Plymouth defences of the 1860s are among the most extensive of the Victorian period.

MEDIEVAL AND LATER FORTIFICATIONS

Barnstaple Castle Mound, Barnstaple.

The tree-clad Castle Mound and trace of a moat are all that remains of a motte and bailey with a shell-keep at the confluence of the Yeo and Taw rivers. The builder may have been Judhael of Totnes, who also founded a Cluniac priory before dying in about 1123. By 1139 it was in the hands of the Tracy family. The castle overlooked the town but had no greater significance.

Berry Pomeroy Castle, Berry Pomeroy, near Totnes.

Impressively sited on a steep wooded spur above the Gatcombe Brook, one mile (1.6 km) north-east of Berry Pomeroy village, the site was originally founded by Ralph de Pomeroy after the Conquest, but the main fortifications were added later by Henry de Pomeroy. The oldest part consists of a tall gatehouse with hexagonal towers, two gateways and a curtain wall with tower. In the early seventeenth century the castle came into the hands of the Seymours, Dukes of Somerset, who still own the site. They began a large Tudor mansion, which was never finished. Last occupied in 1688, this roofless ruin is still impressive. After long decay the castle has been the subject of restoration work in the 1980s.

Lydford Castle.

Chudleigh Fort, East-the-Water, Bideford.

This is a five-sided battery built by Parliamentarian forces under Major-General Chudleigh in April 1642, overlooking the Torridge river, Bideford and its bridge. After the First World War the fort and grounds were purchased as a war memorial and a large granite cross was erected here.

Gidleigh Castle, Gidleigh.

A small square tower keep can be seen close to Gidleigh church below the eastern flank of Dartmoor, 2 miles (3.2 km) from Chagford.

Hemyock Castle, Hemyock, Cullompton.

Parts of this castle remain at Hemyock near the head of the lovely Culm valley, separated from the church by a small stream. One can see the silted-up moat and parts of the outer walls with two round towers. The east gateway gives access to a private residence, although the grounds are open to the public at times. The Parliamentarians used the castle as a prison in the Civil War.

Lydford Castle, Lydford, Okehampton. English Heritage.

This was first built in about 1195 as a prison for the Stannary Courts which held sway over the Dartmoor district. In the thirteenth century a ditch was dug and the spoil piled around the ground floor, the upper part being rebuilt to form the well preserved square tower on a mound seen today. A bailey was also added. The grassy banks of an early Norman fort lie at the south-west tip of the promontory beyond the church. Even earlier, the earthwork defences of the Saxon *burh* surround this western end of the village (see chapter 10).

Marisco Castle, Lundy.

William de Marisco was executed for an attempt on the life of Henry III, and his family's island stronghold replaced by a square keep for the new Constable in 1243. The castle is above the landing beach at the south of the island and has been much altered since, including nineteenth-century cottages within. A bastion to the east was probably added by the Royalists during the Civil War, and Benson's Cave below the castle may have served as a strongroom for their supposed mint. Other defences on Lundy are more coastal. Mangonel Battery above Jenny's Cove could be a de Marisco work, while the more substantial Brazen Ward on the east coast may be of the Elizabethan or Civil War periods.

Okehampton Castle, Okehampton. English Heritage.

Baldwin de Brionne, Sheriff of Devon, built the first castle here soon after the Conquest and encouraged the growth of Okehampton on a site between the West and East Okement rivers. The motte had a stone tower and timber buildings, surrounded by rock-cut ditches and a bank and ditch on the western approach. The history of the castle is one of changing ownership, passing from time to time into royal hands. In 1172 it passed to the

Courtenays, and much of the angular and tottering masonry seen today belongs to the early fourteenth century, when the castle was rebuilt by Hugh Courtenay II. This includes the gatehouse, barbican and north curtain wall on an elongated site to the east of the motte with its enlarged square keep. The Courtenays forfeited the castle in 1538 when Henry Courtenay, Marquis of Exeter, was tried and executed for conspiracy. The castle was abandoned rather than deliberately dismantled.

Plymouth Castle, Barbican, Plymouth.

A small limestone wall of the eastern port is the last remnant of Plymouth's Castle 'Quadrant', overlooking the Barbican and Mayflower Steps from the bottom of Lambhay Street.

Plympton Castle, Plympton St Maurice. Plymouth City Council.

A good motte and bailey survives just west of the church at Plympton St Maurice. On the motte, the much ruined stone shell-keep had timber reinforcements within its walls. It was built in about 1139 by Baldwin de Redvers after the earlier castle had been destroyed when he rebelled against Stephen. Another owner, Fawkes de Bréauté, rebelled against

Henry III in 1224 when there was a fifteen-day siege. The castle returned to the de Redvers before passing in 1297 to Hugh Courtenay (later Earl of Devon). It was unoccupied by the early sixteenth century. During the eighteenth and nineteenth centuries the almost rectangular bailey was used for fairs and circuses.

Rougemont Castle, Castle Street, Exeter.

The castle was built by William soon after the Conquest on a small hill at the north corner of Exeter city wall. The gatehouse is one of the earliest Norman buildings in Britain and its triangular windows show that Saxon masons worked here. The other surviving part is the so-called Athelstan's Tower of the late twelfth century, with a turret added three centuries later. They overlook Rougemont Gardens, which were created in the moat. The County Court was erected in 1774 on the site of the inner bailey.

Royal Citadel, The Hoe, Plymouth. (Contact Plymouth Regional Guides, telephone: 0752 660582.)

This well preserved fortification dates from 1666, when it was begun to the designs of *The blocked gateway of Rougemont Castle, Exeter.*

Okehampton Castle.

Bernard de Gomme, the chief military engineer of Charles II. It is on the site of Drake's earlier fort at the east end of the Hoe, overlooking the entrance to the Cattewater and Sutton Pool. Its dual purpose was to protect the port and control Plymouth, which had been anti-Royalist throughout the Civil War. The main defences are on an irregular plan with projecting bastions on the landward side. A mistake in the design was to carry the masonry up to the parapets, impressive but unable to absorb cannonballs as an earthwork would, and it is as well that the Citadel was never attacked. A very fine baroque portal of 1670 leads to the interior, where buildings are arranged around a parade ground. The royal chapel of St Katherine-upon-the-Hoe is still in use. A lower battery was built close to the shore of Plymouth Sound. In total 160 guns made up the defences. The Citadel is still occupied by the military, but visits can be booked with Plymouth Regional Guides.

Tiverton Castle, Tiverton EX16 6RP. Telephone: 0884 253200.

A castle was built in 1106 by Richard de Redvers, the first Earl of Devon, but rebuilt in the fourteenth century. Activity came to an abrupt end in 1643 when Fairfax took the town and castle and had much destroyed. The notable gatehouse and south-east and south-west towers survive, as do the ruins of the chapel, solar and curtain walls. A mansion was built within the walls soon after the Restoration, and displays include Civil War arms and armour and the Campbell International Clock Collection.

Totnes Castle, Totnes. Telephone: 0803 864406. English Heritage.

A motte and bailey had been built by 1086 by Judhael de Totnes, who also founded a Benedictine priory at Totnes. Two years later the castle was granted to Roger de Nonant, and its later history is one of confiscations and new ownership. The earliest shell-keep on the motte was probably erected by Reginald de Braose, but the castle had been poorly maintained when it was rebuilt in the early fourteenth century. The crenellated shell-keep on its great motte stands prominently above the town, and within are the stone foundations of a square timber tower of the late eleventh century. To the north the inner bailey wall which surrounded the living quarters now encloses a lawn with mature trees. Beyond are a ditch and lesser outer bailey earthwork from the earliest phase. The town walls of Totnes abut on to the castle and the arch of the north gate survives nearby.

COASTAL CASTLES AND DEFENCES

Notable coastal defences were built at Dartmouth and Plymouth. The fortifications at Dartmouth were already in place when Henry VIII embarked on a plan for coastal defence, but in his time Fort Charles was built at the entrance to Salcombe harbour. 'Bulwarks' were also built at the important anchorage of Brixham. Cottages off Overgang Road stand on the foundations of one, and there are other possible sites at Battery Grounds near Fishcombe, and the Round Top or Castle Battery near Berry Head. The most important defensive works were those known as Palmerston's follies, built in the 1860s to defend Plymouth and the naval dockyard at Devonport from a possible French invasion. A minor work of this period was the Old Battery added at Dartmouth Castle.

Bayard's Cove Fort, Dartmouth. English Heritage.

The Dartmouth Corporation built this small artillery fort in 1509-10 to protect the inner harbour mouth. It is a tiny rounded slate-built fort cut back into the rock. The single storey has eleven gunports and a wall walk.

Berry Head Fortifications, near Brixham.

Berry Head (see chapter 2) was heavily fortified during the Napoleonic Wars. The Half Moon Battery had been placed at the extreme head in the 1790s, but the major defences were built in 1803-5. Only two of the three planned forts were built. The main one, Number 3, has an impressive limestone and granite rampart wall with gunports which cut off 16 acres (6.5 ha) of the headland, on the site of an iron age promontory fort. There was a dry moat and entrance was by a drawbridge. The northern part has been quarried away but structures within include the magazine (now the base for the coastguard station), an octagonal sentry box for four and an artillery store. The main guardhouse is now a café. Number 1 fort, the Old Redoubt, has a similar defence surrounding the top of Durl Point. Inside are the magazine and traces of the guardhouse and kitchens. The remains of the small Hardy's Head or Four-Gun Battery can be seen on the north side of the head. No longer required, the forts were dismantled in about 1820. There was renewed activity here with some gun emplacements and observation posts during the Second World War. Berry Head House was built in 1809 as the garrison hospital. It was later the home of the Reverend Henry Francis Lyte and is now a hotel.

Dartmouth Castle, Dartmouth. Telephone: 08043 3588. English Heritage.

Following a French raid on this part of the coast, a fort was built in 1388 by the townspeople of Dartmouth when the merchant John Hawley was mayor. The high curtain wall and

Early nineteenth-century fortifications at Berry Head.

ruined tower behind the car park are all that remains. The main castle was begun in 1481 and was the first in Britain designed for artillery, with gunports commanding the harbour entrance. As extra defence, a chain was hung across to Kingswear Castle on the other side. There is a square tower with round tower attached and flanking gun platforms. The main basement was cut into the rock to house guns, while the two floors above were for accommodation. These now contain exhibitions on the history of coastal defences. There were repairs and additions in the sixteenth century. After a one-month siege at the start, the castle was held by the Royalists throughout the Civil War. A fortified earthwork with projecting bastions was built on the hill behind at Gallant's Bower but was captured with the castle and town by Fairfax in 1646.

On the seaward side was the sixteenth-century Lamberd's Bulwark, a gun battery later rebuilt in 1747 as Maiden Fort. Upon it the Old Battery was built in the 1860s. This Victorian fort had accommodation, magazines and five guns, three in casemates. A large gun can be seen in one of the two positions on the roof. In 1940 this fort was used again with two 4.7 inch (118 mm) guns. A crenellated brick lookout was built on top. The confined site at Dartmouth Castle is complex, for the church (St Petrox) is just behind. A crenellated tower in keeping with the castle is a disused harbour lighthouse, erected in the nineteenth century.

Drake's Island, Plymouth Sound.

St Nicholas or Drake's Island lies strategic-ally off the Hoe at the entrance to the Hamoaze and Tamar estuary. It has been a fortress and after the Restoration a prison for Plymouth's Parliamentarian supporters. Earlier fortifications on the seaward side were strengthened by Sir Francis Drake, and additions were made in 1701, but the greatest works here were the granite casemates built in 1860-4. Intended for 21 guns, they were never fully armed. There are also concrete gun emplacements built in the First World War. The island is now an adventure training centre but can be visited by ferry.

Fort Bovisand, Staddon Point, Wembury.

A single tier of granite casemates for 24 heavy guns was built in 1861-70 to control the entrance to Plymouth Sound in conjunction with the Breakwater Fort and Fort Pickle-combe on the Cornish shore opposite. The fort and its garrison accommodation are now home for the Fort Bovisand Underwater Centre, a diving school.

Fort Charles, Salcombe.

A small fort was built by Henry VIII on the west side of the Salcombe estuary, opposite rocks in the entrance channel. It was held for the King during a four-month blockade at the end of the Civil War. All that remains is broken walls and part of a round corner on a rocky ledge which can be reached at low tide from the cove at North Sands.

Kingswear Castle, Kingswear. Landmark Trust.

This square tower was begun in 1491 to complement Dartmouth Castle on the opposite shore, from which it can be seen. With improved guns installed at Dartmouth able to cover the whole harbour entrance, Kingswear Castle became obsolete and was abandoned in the seventeenth century. In 1855 Charles Seale-Hayne bought and converted the castle into a residence. It was purchased in 1987 by the Landmark Trust for conversion to holiday flats.

Mount Batten Tower, Turnchapel, near Plymouth.

A round gun tower of 1664 can be seen on the high knoll opposite Plymouth Royal Citadel at the mouth of the Cattewater. Mount Batten takes its name from Captain Batten, who was stationed here in 1644. In the 1920s the Royal Air Force took over the peninsula as a seaplane base.

Plymouth Breakwater Fort, Plymouth Sound.

This island fort of granite and armour plating was built in 1861-70 just inside the Plymouth Breakwater, where it is a prominent feature. It is of the same period and purpose as the forts in the Spithead at Portsmouth. Improved firepower from shore batteries rendered the fort obsolete, but it remained important as an observation and signal station.

Plymouth Defences, Plymouth.

As part of the 1860s defences, ten forts and batteries were erected around the north side of Plymouth to protect the city and naval dockyard from a landward attack. Once in open country, they are now within the city suburbs and three can be seen easily from the former ring road. Bowden Battery is now a garden centre, and Woodlands Fort has an impressive main gateway arch. Between the two and slightly north is the larger Crownhill Fort. There were other land fortifications on the east side of the Sound, where the large Fort Stamford (now the Plymouth Leisure Centre) is an impressive structure overlooking the Cattewater and visible from Plymouth Hoe. The fort on Staddon Heights is surrounded by a golf course, while Fort Bovisand is on the shore. Completing the ring were other forts on the Cornish side of the haven.

Plymouth Dock Lines, Devonport.

Strong defences with projecting bastions were built to protect the naval dockyard at Plymouth Dock (later renamed Devonport). Work began in 1756, but after many interruptions the scheme took a century to complete, by which time the dockyard was expanding far outside. A good section survives overlooking the bridge at Stonehouse Creek.

The church of St Michael at Brentor.

30

5
Churches

Atherington: St Mary.

This north Devon village church is noted for its screen with a unique rood loft, beautifully carved. There are effigies of Sir Ralph Wilmington (died 1349) and his wife, a rather worn earlier one of Sir William Champernowne, and brasses of Sir John Bassett (died 1529), his two wives and twelve children.

Aveton Gifford: St Andrew.

Destroyed by enemy bombing with much of the village in December 1943, the church was rebuilt to a solid cruciform plan with a low central tower (rebuilt twice). The plain modern altar table is effective. The multi-arched north porch survives from the thirteenth-century church. Below is the village at the head of the Avon estuary, where there is a causeway and a tidal road to Bigbury.

Berry Pomeroy: St Mary.

The church was rebuilt in the late fifteenth century by Sir Richard Pomeroy, whose family had owned the estate since the Conquest. The south porch has a good stone-vaulted roof and within is a screen with painted panels. The Seymour Chapel has a monument to Sir Edward Seymour (son of the Lord Protector Somerset, who bought the estate from the Pomeroys) and his son Lord Edward (died 1613) with his wife and eleven children. All three recline on steps, while nine children kneel below, with one imbecile daughter in a chair and one in a cradle. This is a peaceful location overlooking fields next to the manor house at the edge of the small village. The castle (see chapter 4) lies one mile (1.6 km) away.

Bishopsteignton: St John the Baptist.

Overlooking the Teign estuary, the chief interest is outside, where a Norman west doorway has carvings still clear-cut, and the blocked south door has a tympanum depicting the Adoration of the Magi. The tower of 1815 has a copied Norman doorway. About a mile (1.6 km) north, up Old Walls Hill, are the remains of the summer palace of the Bishops of Exeter, enlarged by Bishop Grandisson in 1332. The end of a red sandstone range with lancet windows can be seen among farm buildings beside the road.

Brentor: St Michael.

At a spectacular site on the distinctive volcanic rock of Brent Tor between Lydford and Tavistock, this is the fourth smallest complete church in England and dates from the twelfth century with later rebuilding. From this windswept place there are far views across Dartmoor and much of the Devon and Cornwall border lands.

Broadclyst: St John.

The grand late fifteenth-century tower of volcanic stone is lichen-encrusted. Within, the large church has two Beer stone arcades with carved capitals. One of the treasures is part of an illuminated mass, cut up to bind an account book of 1581. Among the monuments is an ornate one to Sir John Acland (died 1613) and his two wives, for Broadclyst was part of the Aclands' Killerton estate (see chapter 6). The church is across a field from the village, which has thatched cottages and stone almshouses. There is an old windmill tower outside the village (see chapter 8).

Buckfast Abbey: St Mary.

This is the church of a Benedictine monastery built in Norman and Gothic styles by the monks from 1907 to 1938. More has been added since, including stained glass in the east window and a modern chapel. An exhibition and audio-visual show trace the abbey's long history from the first building of 1018, re-founded by the Cistercians in 1147. The Benedictines came here in 1882, taking over a mansion of 1805 built from the abbey stones. Buckfast honey and tonic wine are for sale and a textile mill and shop are adjacent to the site.

Cadeleigh: St Bartholomew.

Almost lost in hilly country but worth finding, the church feels ancient. The single arcade has foliage and heads carved on the capitals, and there are box pews. Most splendid is a tall ornate canopied monument to Sir Symon Leach and his family, erected in 1630. In front of the monument are old floor tiles. The south porch, restored in 1922, has corbelled heads of King George V and Queen Mary.

Cheriton Bishop: St Mary.

On a hill at the north edge of the village, a haven from the busy A30, the tower is of granite ashlar, but the church body is a reddish stone with a leaning chancel wall. A carved fifteenth-century alabaster fragment was found when rebuilding the south wall in 1884. The screen of 1520 in the north aisle has painted panels, and there is a squat decorated Norman font.

Chittlehampton: St Hieritha.

The church has a handsome early sixteenth-century tower 114 feet (35 metres) high, standing over a sloping village square flanked with thatched cottages. The south porch is approached through an arched tunnel of limes.

Buckfast Abbey.

Within are bare stone walls and arcades of Beer and Dundry stone. The stone pulpit of about 1500 has carved figures including St Hieritha. In the north transept or Giffard Chapel is a fine monument to John Giffard (died 1622) and other family members.

Cornworthy: St Peter.

Here are granite pillars and Beer stone arches, Georgian box pews and a pulpit with sounding board. The plain walls are broken by a painted stone memorial of 1611 to Sir Thomas Harris, his wife and four children; one of these, Christopher, was slain in the wars at Zealand in Flanders. Nearby a wall tablet to Lucy Spurway is curious. Just west of the village is the ruined fourteenth-century gateway of St Mary's, an Augustinian priory of nuns founded in 1231-8.

Crediton: Holy Cross.

There was a Saxon cathedral at Crediton until the see was moved to Exeter in 1050. The large church is mainly of red sandstone, in a cruciform plan with a central tower on Norman piers. It was a collegiate church of the twelfth century, rebuilt in about 1410. At the Dissolution, the town bought it as the parish church for £200, and since then it has been maintained by twelve governors. The Governors' Room can be visited, where there is

also a small museum containing relics from the Civil War. The Lady Chapel of about 1300 was a grammar school from 1572 until 1860. The east window of 1897 includes events from the life and martyrdom of St Boniface, born at Crediton in AD 640. Monuments include a knight and his lady, the former believed to be Sir John Sully, who died in 1387 aged 105. There is also Sir William Peryam, judge of Mary, Queen of Scots. Most impressive is the richly ornamented arch in memory of Sir Redvers Henry Buller, who was born at Downes outside the town. He won the Victoria Cross in the Zulu War and raised the siege of Ladysmith when he was commander-in-chief in the Boer War.

Cullompton: St Andrew.

The wool trade financed much of this fine town church, with its tall elaborate tower of the mid sixteenth century. The body of the church dates from 1430, and the clerestory gives light to the interior with its Beer stone arcades and painted roofs. There is a good painted rood screen, but also preserved is the original medieval base of the rood, with bones and skulls carved in ancient oak as hard as stone. A Jacobean timber gallery is supported by Ionic columns. The south aisle was added in 1526 by the wool merchant John Lane and has fan vaulting inside and rich carvings outside.

Culmstock: All Saints.

A yew tree grows from the top of the embattled tower. Within, the two arcades are of Beer and Ham stone. A Morris and Burne-Jones window of 1896 is a memorial to the Corner family. A beautiful cope made at nearby Prescott in about 1490 has been carefully restored and displayed. R. D. Blackmore's father was priest in charge here in about 1820. Frederick Temple, Archbishop of Canterbury, 1896 to 1902, taught in the church Sunday school.

Dalwood: Loughwood Meeting House.

This small buttressed chapel at Loughwood Farm, close to the A35 between Axminster and Honiton, was built in about 1653 and contains box pews and a gallery of the early eighteenth century. The National Trust cares for the building.

Dartmouth: St Saviour.

This is a gem of a church. The ornate rood screen dates from the late fifteenth century and has painted panels with saints. The sixteenth-century altar has carved figures of saints and the carved and painted stone pulpit is wineglass-shaped. A good brass on the chancel floor is to John Hauley (died 1408) and his two wives. Chaucer's Shipman is said to have been based on this Dartmouth merchant. There is also a charming small brass of a lady. The gallery is dated 1633 and the arms of Charles II were placed here on his restoration. The south door is dated 1631, but the fine ironwork is perhaps late fourteenth-century. The strap hinges across the door are in the form of tree foliage guarded by two beasts.

Dunkeswell Abbey

A Cistercian abbey was founded here in the Madford valley in 1201. Of the few ruins, the gatehouse is partly incorporated in Abbey Cottage, while parts of the west range are among farm buildings. Holy Trinity church (1842) is over the nave and contains a small display on the abbey and Cistercians. There are two richly carved Norman fonts in the neighbouring churches, at Dunkeswell 2 miles (3.2 km) south and at Luppitt in an adjoining valley.

East Budleigh: All Saints.

The church stands above a street of thatched cottages. There are two Beer stone arcades, one pillar having a lesser capital and carved face. Furnishings include old bench ends and an elaborately carved pulpit with figures in biblical scenes. There is a modern memorial to Sir Walter Raleigh, who was born nearby at Hayes Barton in 1552. His father was a churchwarden and he worshipped here as a boy. Outside is a good churchyard, and a

simple stone near the south porch is to three children of Henry and Isabella Gardner, none of whom lived for more than five months.

Ermington: St Peter and St Paul.

Here is a famous crooked spire of the early fourteenth century, rebuilt in the 1850s. One of several legends has it that the spire bowed to a beautiful lady on her wedding day but failed to straighten up afterwards! The body of the church is of the fifteenth and sixteenth centuries, restored in 1889. The pulpit was carved mainly by Miss Violet Pinwell, whose father was vicar from 1880 to 1924. Other work designed by her includes an alabaster relief of the Nativity. A canopied tomb in the south chapel has painted heraldic shields of about 1580, believed to be for William Strachleigh or his son-in-law Christopher Chudleigh.

Exeter Cathedral: St Peter.

Exeter is one of the great English cathedrals, richly decorated and with much to see. The original Saxon cathedral of 1050 was rebuilt by the Normans under Bishop Warelwast. Only the two towers remain over the north and south transepts of the present cathedral, which was begun in 1260. Much Beer stone was used for the interior work.

The leaning spire at Ermington.

During his tenure from 1327 to 1369, Bishop Grandisson completed the west front and nave. The former has statues of kings and saints and a fine window. The superb Gothic vaulted nave is the longest of its kind. There is a minstrels' gallery on the north side, while the north transept contains a clock of 1376. The south transept has the chapel of St John the Baptist with a fifteenth-century throne and gilt canopy. More renowned is the Bishop's Throne in the choir, carved in wood in 1316 for Bishop Stapledon with an exceptionally tall canopy. The choir stalls have thirteenth-century misericords, and the roof has notable carved bosses. The organ stands majestically above the choir screen of 1320-4. There are many tombs of bishops and the Lady Chapel includes those of Leofric, the first Bishop, and Branscombe, who began the Norman cathedral. Grandisson is buried in a small chapel within the west front. Outside, the Bishop's Palace has a library with medieval manuscripts and its grounds are open to those accompanied by tourist guides.

Hartland: St Nectan.

The church is at Stoke, west of Hartland village and near the sea. The 128 foot (39 metre) pinnacled tower is a landmark for

The figure of St Nectan on the church tower at Hartland.

sailors and has a carved figure of St Nectan on one wall. Although mainly of about 1460, the large church has a late twelfth-century Norman font with carved heads. The rood screen is 45 feet (13.7 metres) long and has never been restored. The altar was made in 1931 as a war memorial and has carved figures of saints of the ancient chapels of Hartland. The Lady Chapel is notable for its beautiful roof and fourteenth-century glass. The Pope's Chamber was occupied by the priest but now contains church relics. Hartland Abbey is open to the public (see chapter 6).

Kenton: All Saints.

This late fourteenth-century church has a superb exterior and tower in red sandstone. The carved and painted screen of 1455 has forty panels painted with saints and prophets. Of similar date is the elaborately carved oak pulpit, discarded in the nineteenth century but restored by Reverend Sabine Baring-Gould. This may be an old site for there is a tradition that St Petrock established a chapel here in about AD 560.

Lewtrenchard: St Peter.

This small church has seventeenth-century brasses and big slate slabs to the Goulds, for the nearby manor, now a hotel, was the family home for many years. The Reverend Sabine Baring-Gould was rector from 1881 until his death in 1924. He and his grandfather before him restored the church, which remains attractive with wagon roof, screen and original bench ends. **Bratton Clovelly** is 3½ miles (5.6 km) north, where its hilltop church has traces of Norman work and wall paintings.

Marystow: St Mary the Virgin.

The church stands alone on a hilltop overlooking Chillaton village to the south. Indications of a Norman church are a square Norman font with carved corner heads, and the remains of an arch over the south door. The chief interest is the monument to Sir Thomas Wyse (1629), extraordinary for such a remote church. The effigies of Wyse and his wife lie with a son and daughter kneeling at the head, a seated toddler and two infants in cots. Sir Thomas was knighted at the coronation of James I and rebuilt the nearby family manor house of Sydenham.

Molland: St Mary.

Inside is a single low arcade of Beer stone with carved capitals, box pews and uneven floor. Outside, beasts crouch at the corners of the tower. Against the south wall is a memorial to eight members of the Pincombe family, drowned with 187 fellow emigrants when wrecked on the Manacles in 1855 six hours out from Plymouth for Quebec. Their ship was the

The twin-towered church at Ottery St Mary.

barque *John*, whose negligent captain was sentenced for manslaughter.

Newton St Cyres: St Julitta and St Cyres.

This mainly fifteenth-century church is of local volcanic stone. Carved bosses in the roof of the south porch have faces and a sow with piglets. Plain windows illuminate the interior, where the painted Beer stone arcade has carved capitals. There is a superb seventeenth-century monument with most of the original colours showing, at an angle in the north aisle. It is to Sir John Northcote, who died at Hayne in 1632, and includes the heads of his father, grandfather and two wives (he had eighteen children by his second wife, Susanna). It was erected in 1637 by his son, whose effigy kneels at the base with his wife and children. This second Sir John was member for the county throughout the Long Parliament. Also of note is a small effigy of Sherland Shore, who died in 1632 aged seventeen.

Ottery St Mary: St Mary.

As at Exeter Cathedral, this beautiful church has flanking towers, one with a spire. It was well restored by William Butterfield in the 1840s and retains many interesting features. Bishop Grandisson of Exeter made it a collegiate church in 1334 and rebuilt the nave and Lady Chapel, the latter with figured roof bosses. Parclose screens and a clock in the south transept date from this time. There is also a rare gilded wooden eagle lectern. In the nave are tombs with effigies of Otto de Grandisson and his wife, Beatrice (died 1358 and 1374). The Dorset aisle was added in 1520 by the Marchioness of Dorset and has a superb fan-vaulted ceiling.

Parracombe: St Petrock.

In Churchtown at the top of the scattered village, this redundant church has been preserved. The tower and nave are thirteenth-century and there are bench ends and box pews from later centuries. The church was replaced by a Victorian one in the main village.

Sidbury: St Giles and St Peter.

This interesting church stands on an ancient site, for there is a Saxon crypt. The Norman tower has a vaulted base with four large corbels carved with heads: a man and beast. The top of the tower was rebuilt by the Victorians, who added a shingle spire. The rest of the church is mainly thirteenth-century with a restoration of 1445. The nave and two aisles have wagon roofs and elaborate carved side arches, and there are traces of a painting above the chancel arch. The carved octagonal font is unusual for having an old lock plate. A

The remarkable carvings on the Greenway Chapel at St Peter's church, Tiverton.

gallery of 1754 supports the organ. The part-Tudor Court House overlooks the church and there are attractive cottages with thatch in this village of the Sid valley.

Silverton: St Mary the Virgin.
The church is crenellated outside. The mostly clear-glass windows give a spacious feel to the interior, where there are two arcades of Beer stone with carved capitals and a wagon roof with painted bosses. One carved boss is in remembrance of Cardinal Bourne, chaplain to Mary Tudor until banished to Silverton upon the succession of Elizabeth. The organ is supported by a timber gallery on pillars, dated 1734, with panels listing benefactions for the poor. The village, at the meeting of roads, is not unattractive.

South Milton: All Saints.
The sea is within sight, 1½ miles (2.4 km) down the valley from this church, with its buttressed tower and low arched south porch. Inside there are bare stone walls, a single Beer stone arcade carved on the mouldings, wagon roofs and an unusual low screen. The round Norman font has heads, birds, an ox and a heavy rope ornament.

South Tawton: St Andrew.
This large granite church has a tall fifteenth-century tower. It is a surprise to step down inside to find two arcades of white Beer stone in a district so close to the Dartmoor granite, suggesting past wealth brought by the wool trade. There are two notable monuments. In the north aisle is the effigy of John Wykes (died 1592), lying recumbent with his feet on a duck. In the Lady Chapel statuettes of Robert Burgoyne and his wife kneel above a slate slab with their children, eight kneeling, one in a cot and one in swaddling clothes, dated 1651. Outside the churchyard is the granite and thatched Church House, with double stairs to the upper floor forming an arch over the main door. In contrast, St Peter's church in the larger village of **North Tawton** has a low tower and shingle spire with an external sanctus bell. Outside is a Roman granite pillar.

Spicelands: Friends' Meeting House.
Spicelands is halfway between Culmstock and Uffculme on the north side of the river Culm. It was established between 1679 and 1683 as possibly the first Friends' meeting house in Devon. The original cob and thatched building was replaced in 1815 by the present one in stone and slate, which is attached to a house. Within, the benches and balcony are in plain pine. The simple burial ground had 113 burials up to 1884 and contains some head-stones.

Stowford: St John.

The late fourteenth-century church was restored by Sir Giles Gilbert Scott in 1872-4, but a stone by the gate carved in the ogham script with the name Gunglei suggests an early site at this small hamlet. The tower has banded granite and slate courses, and granite arcades and wagon roofs inside. Of most interest are the monuments to the Harris family of Haine. These include Christopher Harris (died 1718) and John Harris (died 1767), the latter described as 'a kind master exemplary in sobriety and good order in his family'.

Tiverton: St Peter.

The church reflects the riches brought to the town by the wool trade. In 1517 the merchant John Greenway added the south porch and chapel. Among the rich carvings outside is a frieze depicting period sailing ships. Inside are brasses of Greenway and his wife Joan. The church interior is large, with three aisles and side chapels, but has been much affected by restoration. In the chancel are the tombs of wool merchants and almshouse builders John Walrond (1579) and George Slee (1613), the latter a massive tomb-chest with a black limestone top. The mayor's pew has a plaster lion and unicorn and a prayer book of 1750. Two huge paintings hang in the church: local Richard Cosway's 'St Peter in Prison', and Gasper de Craeyer's 'The Magi'.

Torbryan: Holy Trinity.

The mortar-washed church is in a lovely setting by a farm, cottages and the fifteenth-century Church House Inn. It was built in about 1400 and the screen with its panels painted with saints dates from thirty years later. The pulpit is made from parts of the original screen, and the altar from the original pulpit. Ancient stained glass is preserved in the upper windows. The valley is not far from **Ipplepen**, whose tall church tower is a prominent landmark.

Torquay: All Saints.

Beside Cary Park at Babbacombe, this church was designed in the Gothic style by William Butterfield in 1865. The dark interior is rich in polished stones, with walls and round pillars of black, red and white marbles. The elaborate font is also marble, but the walls of the sanctuary are lined with polished alabaster up to the string course.

Torquay: St John the Apostle.

This church by G. E. Street overlooks the harbour from Montpelier Terrace. It has east and west windows designed by Burne-Jones.

Torquay: St Mary.

The church with its pinnacled tower is on the highest point of the town, surrounded by a churchyard at St Marychurch. It was bombed on 30th May 1943, killing 26 children and teachers, but was rebuilt ten years later. A good Norman font remains from the old church, carved with beasts, a drinking hunter, horseman and harpist. Almost adjacent is the Catholic church of Our Lady Help of Christians and St Denis. It is of grey limestone with a spire, to the design of J. Hansom and Son in 1865. These two prominent churches make a striking landmark above the surrounding urban development.

Torquay: St Saviour.

This was the church of Tor Mohun, the earlier village north-east of Torre Abbey and now Torquay. The interior was over-restored in 1849 but contains the tomb of Thomas Cary (died 1567), whose descendants were to help develop the resort.

Totnes: St Mary.

The mid fifteenth-century red sandstone tower is 120 feet (36.6 metres) high. On a projecting stair turret and south buttresses are very corroded figures of Bishop Lacy, a knight and Mary with child. Inside are four aisles and a grand screen of Beer stone. In St George's Chapel is the canopied tomb-chest of Sir Walter Smythe (died 1555), who founded the King Edward VI Grammar School. On the north aisle wall effigies of Christopher Blackhall (died 1633) and his four wives kneel to the right (east). In the nave are the Corporation pews of 1636. Two late seventeenth-century bibles are preserved, presented by Sir Edward and Lady Anne Seymour of Berry Pomeroy Castle (see chapter 4).

Uffculme: St Mary.

A grey limestone tower with spire locates the church in this attractive working village. Within, a very fine fifteenth-century screen crosses the four aisles and full width of this broad church. The pulpit of 1719 has an added sixteenth-century Flemish carving of the Ascension. In the Walrond Chapel is a painted tomb-chest of 1663 for William Walrond, and a bewigged figure in armour reclining on a window ledge is probably Sir William Walrond (died 1689).

A la Ronde, the round house at Exmouth.

6
Historic buildings and gardens

Devon has a great variety of historic houses, but by no means all are open to the public. For example, **Hayes Barton** is largely unaltered since the birth here of Sir Walter Raleigh in 1552. It offers farmhouse accommodation and can be seen from a lane one mile (1.6 km) west of East Budleigh. Just north of Colyton, the National Trust allows limited access to **Shute Barton**, a crenellated house with a striking gatehouse flanked by smaller pavilions. At the other end of the county, **Wortham Manor** near Lifton has been converted to flats by the Landmark Trust but can be viewed from outside. The impressive mansion and gardens at **Castle Hill**, between Barnstaple and South Molton, are open by appointment only. Some houses described below may not be open every day, so it is always worth checking first to avoid disappointment.

A la Ronde, Summer Lane, Exmouth EX8 5BD. Telephone: 0395 265514.

Two spinster cousins, Jane and Mary Parminter, planned and built this unique house in 1794 on returning from a ten-year Grand Tour of Europe.

Inspired by the sixth-century church of San Vitale in Ravenna, which has sixteen sides and an octagonal nave, they designed their house in the same shape but disguised it as a rustic cottage with a thatched roof (now tiled). Its twenty rooms radiate from a central octagon, high above which is the Shell Gallery, which is reached through two Gothic grottoes. The drawing room is decorated with a frieze and dado of birds' feathers and pictures made from sand, seaweed and paper. Much of the original furniture remains. A la Ronde is set in parkland with glimpses of the Exe estuary, Berry Head and the south Devon coast. Jane and Mary are buried in Point-in-View, their curious chapel up on the hill behind. It is a low building with a pyramid roof and incorporates four small cottages (formerly almshouses for elderly spinsters) and a school for six orphaned girls. It was built in 1811 but enlarged in 1829 when the nearby Manse was built. The chapel is still in use and is open to the public. A la Ronde remains in the same family.

Arlington Court, near Barnstaple EX31 4LP. Telephone: 027182 296. National Trust.

The house looks across a park down the steep wooded sides of the Yeo valley, 5½ miles (9 km) north-east of Barnstaple. There were Chichesters here from the sixteenth century, but the house dates from 1822. Rather plain outside, it has a curved entrance porch and was greatly enlarged forty years later by the addition of a long wing. Miss Rosalie Chichester left Arlington to the National Trust in 1949, and her large collections of china, pewter and shells are on display. The ship models are very fine, many by French prisoners of war. In contrast is a model of the yacht *Gipsy Moth IV*, in which Sir Francis Chichester sailed around the world, for he was related to the family. Toys are on show in the Day Nursery. The Morning Room has original 1839 paint and wallpaper. Outside is the Victorian garden with azaleas, while Shetland ponies and Jacob sheep graze in the park. A large National Trust collection of horse-drawn vehicles is housed in the stables, and visitors can have carriage rides.

Bickleigh Castle, Bickleigh, near Tiverton EX16 8RP. Telephone: 08845 363.

Bickleigh Castle is on the west bank of the Exe 4 miles (6.4 km) south of Tiverton, near Bickleigh. Of Norman origin, it was owned by the Courtenays in the late fourteenth century, but the Carews came here soon after. In the Civil War it was held by Sir Henry Carew for the Royalists and suffered greatly in an attack

by Fairfax so that little remained except for the gatehouse and chapel. The latter is across the lane from the gatehouse and dates from about 1100. The substantial gatehouse was built in the late fourteenth century on earlier foundations and much altered since. On either side of the arch are the armoury, with a display of weapons and armour, and the guardroom, containing Tudor furniture and a portrait of Queen Henrietta Maria, wife of Charles I. Over the arch is the Great Hall, with panelling and a minstrels' gallery. Behind the gatehouse, the seventeenth-century farmhouse wing became the family home after the destruction of the castle. The dining room was once the farm kitchen and there is a rare bacon-curing chamber next to it. The Garden Room is the old dairy and has a fine carved stone overmantel depicting scenes from the Bible or family history. The thatched barn contains a museum of domestic and agricultural artefacts, dolls' houses and toys. Unusually, there is also a collection of escape and spy equipment from the Second World War. The maritime exhibition includes Tudor ship models and a *Titanic* display: the Fourth Officer was related to the owner of Bickleigh Castle. Of special relevance to Bickleigh is an exhibition on the *Mary Rose*, for Vice Admiral Sir George Carew was

The gatehouse at Bickleigh Castle.

The palm house at Bicton Park.

in command when she sank at Spithead in 1545. The moat has been turned into attractive ponds, part of a formal garden with rhododendrons.

Bicton Park, East Budleigh, Budleigh Salterton. Telephone: 0395 68465.

These splendid gardens are maintained by a charitable trust and are deservedly popular. They form part of the grounds of Lord Henry Rolle's eighteenth-century Bicton House, now an agricultural college. He laid out the formal Italian Gardens with lawns and a lake in 1735. They were walled in 1845. Exotic plants are grown in glasshouses, the finest and earliest being the large Palm House of 1815-20. The American Garden was established in the 1830s, with trees and shrubs brought from the family estates in Florida and the Bahamas. The flint-built Shell House has a collection of shells, many from the Bahamas. There are also a pinetum of rare conifers, the peaceful Hermitage Garden and the Oriental Garden created in the 1980s. Other attractions include an 18 inch (45 cm) gauge Woodland Railway, orchid house, bird garden, exhibitions, entertainments for children and the James Countryside Museum (see chapters 7 and 9).

Bowden House, near Totnes TQ9 7PW. Telephone: 0803 863664.

Bowden House is one mile (1.6 km) south of Totnes on the Ashprington road. Originally the home of the lords of the manor of Totnes, the medieval house was converted to a Tudor brick mansion in the 1520s by John Giles. The present Queen Anne facade and other extensive alterations were made by Nicholas Trist, who bought Bowden in 1704. After passing through several owners and uses, the house is being restored and visitors are shown around by guides in Georgian dress. The Tudor Great Hall, its walls adorned with eighteenth- and nineteenth-century weapons, retains a decorated plaster ceiling of 1510, as does the Grand Hall, decorated in neo-classical baroque style. The Tudor panelled library includes a carved overmantel of 1585, possibly brought here from a house in Exeter. Trist's oak staircase is also of note. There are exhibits about the two Trist brothers who settled in America, where they fought in the War of Independence. A grandson later bought 919,161 square miles (2,380,627 sq km) of land. The British Photographic Museum is housed here (see chapter 7).

Bradley Manor, Newton Abbot TQ12 6BN. National Trust.

This fifteenth-century manor house in the wooded Lemon valley on the western outskirts of Newton Abbot, approached from the A381 Totnes road, was built by Richard and Joan Yarde on the site of an earlier building and altered in later years with, for example, the addition of Gothic windows and features. After becoming dilapidated and converted to estate workers' accommodation in the nineteenth century, Bradley Manor was bought in 1909 by Cecil Firth, who began its restoration. The Great Hall, with timber roof and granite fireplace, has a screens passage with seventeenth-century panelling. Of later improvements, little remains of the fleur-de-lis once stencilled on the walls of the Banqueting Hall, but there is good panelling and an elaborate plaster cornice in the Panelled Room of the late seventeenth century. Beside the house, the chapel of 1427 has roof bosses carved with the arms of the Yardes and the Ferrers, Joan's family.

Buckland Abbey, near Yelverton PL20 6EY. Telephone: 0822 853607. National Trust.

A Cistercian abbey was established here in about 1278. After the Dissolution, in 1541, it was bought by Sir Richard Grenville. His grandson and famous namesake of the *Revenge* lived here and made improvements before moving to Stowe in Cornwall. The property was sold in 1581 to Sir Francis Drake, who became mayor of Plymouth. Later members of his family made alterations to the house. Among the items on display is the famous Drake's Drum, which tradition tells will sound and summon Drake when danger threatens England. There are also letters written by Drake and banners said to have been flown from his *Golden Hinde* when he was knighted in 1581. The Great Hall is Grenville's work and has a good plaster ceiling and a curious frieze showing a knight without armour beside a Tree of Life laden with skulls. The kitchen with its large granite fireplace is another of his improvements. Of the later alterations, the Georgian Room has a Tudor fireplace but Georgian plasterwork and panell-

Buckland Abbey, near Yelverton.

ing. The chapel was the abbey chancel. Another part open is the monks' guesthouse. The fourteenth-century tithe barn is 154 feet (47 metres) long. An exhibition on the history of the abbey was opened in 1988.

Cadhay, Ottery St Mary EX11 1QT. Telephone: 040481 2432.

Cadhay was recorded in about 1300 as a sub-manor to the manor of Ottery St Mary, held by the de Cadehay family. The present house dates mainly from about 1550 when John Haydon used some material brought from Dunkeswell Abbey. An Elizabethan long gallery was added by Robert Haydon, and is 60 feet (18.3 metres) long. The Great Hall survives from an earlier house, but in 1737 an upper floor was put in, later becoming accommodation for farm labourers. Despite this, the roof timbers have survived and may be as early as 1420. The inner courtyard has statues of sovereigns from Henry VIII to Elizabeth I. In the garden there are medieval fish ponds.

Castle Drogo, Drewsteignton, Exeter EX6 6PB. Telephone: 06473 3306. National Trust.

Sir Edwin Lutyens's masterpiece in granite is the last 'castle' to be built in Britain. It stands on a well chosen spur, with superb views down the upper Teign gorge and across to Dartmoor. It was built for Julius Drewe, whose fortune came from developing the Home and Colonial Stores, and whose distant ancestor Drogo de Teigne gave his name to Drewsteignton parish. The foundation stone was laid in 1911, but Lutyens's original ambitious plans were modified in the following

41

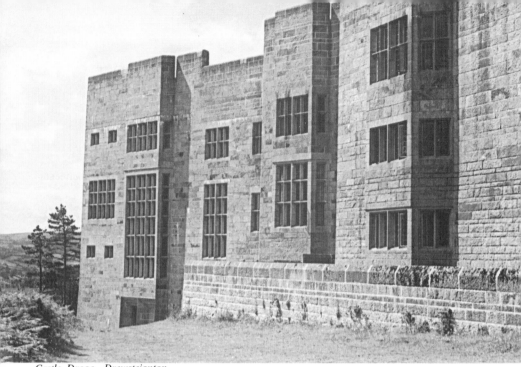

Castle Drogo, Drewsteignton.

year. The work was not completed until 1930, a year before Drewe's death. Granite was used throughout from quarries at nearby Whiddon Park and Dartmoor. A lion and the Drewe motto are carved over the main entrance, which has a portcullis. Inside, bare granite walls are prominent, seen in rooms and the impressive main stairs. Furnishings include tapestries, family portraits and furniture brought from Drewe's former home at Wadhurst Hall in Sussex. Off the Green Corridor are the family's private rooms with excellent views; Adrian Drewe's room was arranged by Mrs Drewe as a memorial to her eldest son, who died in Flanders in 1917. Low down at the south end is the chapel, the last part to be finished. Next to it, the Gun Room has a fascinating collection of architectural drawings and photographs of the construction work. Great yew hedges close to the house continue the effect of a castle wall, while elsewhere in the garden another tall hedge surrounds a large circular lawn. There is access to Whiddon Deer Park, riverside paths and the Hunters Path in the Teign gorge.

Chambercombe Manor, Ilfracombe EX38 9RJ. Telephone: 0271 62624.

Once the home of the Champernons, this twelfth-century manor house was much altered in Tudor times. Several rooms are open to the public. The kitchen has a large open hearth and a lime-ash floor. A similar floor is in the Great Hall, which had an upper floor added to include the Tudor Bedroom, which has a period bed and plaster frieze. It is said to have been prepared for Lady Jane Grey. Above the priest's hole is the Hidden Bedroom, in which was discovered a lady's skeleton lying on a bed, her identity the subject of much speculation, and presumably the manor's ghost. The private chapel dates from at least 1439. There are gardens with ponds, lawns and a herb garden.

Coleton Fishacre Garden, near Kingswear TQ6 0EQ. Telephone: 080425 466. National Trust.

The house of local stone (not open) was completed in 1926 to the design of Oswald Milne for Rupert and Lady Dorothy D'Oyly Carte. Below, 18 acres (7.3 ha) of gardens with terraced grass paths beneath a variety of trees descend steeply in a valley towards the sea. The mild conditions provided by this shelter allow cultivation of unusual plants. The Rill Garden has a wall fountain and a channelled stream which continues through ponds in the informal gardens. A gazebo stands above the quarry, which produced the stone for the house, and gives a view of the sea.

Compton Castle, Marldon, near Paignton TQ3 1TA. Telephone: 08047 2112. National Trust.

One of the best fortified houses in Britain, Compton Castle is stone-built with corner towers and tucked away in a combe 2½ miles (4 km) inland from the coast at Torbay. It was begun in about 1329 by Geoffrey Gilbert and enlarged around 1450. Further defences were added in about 1520, when there was danger of French raids. The Gilberts left Compton Castle in about 1750 and sold it fifty years later. It was bought back in a ruinous condition in 1930 and the long task of restoration began. The National Trust continues this work although the castle is still occupied by the family. It is entered through a portcullised entrance in a high wall before crossing a court to the Great Hall. This was reconstructed in 1954-5 and has a screens passage with a minstrels' gallery above. There are family portraits of famous Elizabethan seafarers: Sir Humphrey Gilbert colonised Newfoundland in 1583, and his eldest son Sir John Gilbert was with his uncle Sir Walter Raleigh on a Guiana expedition and knighted for his part in the sacking of Cadiz in 1596. The younger son, Raleigh Gilbert, led an attempt to found the Sagadahoc colony in Maine, 1607-8. There is a model of the *Squirrel*, which was lost off the Azores with Sir Humphrey when returning from Newfoundland. A later Sir Walter Raleigh Gilbert was a major-general who achieved fame in the Indian Sikh Wars in the 1840s. The restored chapel has modern pews with carved squirrels and family arms. Other parts open include the old kitchen. The whole is surrounded by a high wall, and a great thatched eighteenth-century barn stands on the west side at the front. Opposite is the Rose Garden, which contains an armillary sphere made in 1983 to commemorate the four hundredth anniversary of the colonisation of Newfoundland.

Dartington Hall, near Totnes.

Dartington Hall, Dartington, Totnes TQ9 6EL. Telephone: 0803 862271.

The estate and dilapidated former medieval manor house of the Duke of Exeter were purchased in 1925 by Leonard and Dorothy Elmhirst, and the Dartington Trust was established six years later. The buildings were restored and the site developed to include an arts centre (now the Dartington College of Arts), a progressive co-educational school (now closed) and other commercial activities. The centrepiece is the restored fourteenth-century Great Hall, now the venue for concerts. A central boss over the entrance porch has a white hart on a rose, the emblem of Richard II, who gave the manor to his half-brother John Holland. However, the Champernownes lived here from Elizabethan times to the twentieth century. The hall is part of a range of old buildings around a grass quadrangle, approached through an arch. The tower of the old church is just north of the hall. The surrounding landscaped gardens have been laid out with grass terraces and sculptures, including a fine Henry Moore reclining figure.

Elizabethan House, 32 New Street, Plymouth. Telephone: 0752 264878. Plymouth City Council.

In one of the Barbican's narrow streets, the house of an Elizabethan sea captain has been restored, with period furniture, some of which has been loaned by the Victoria and Albert Museum. It includes a front room and kitchen with a side passage to a small courtyard and garden at the rear. A spiral staircase leads to two upper floors. Plymouth City Council owns this and the Merchant's House, which is also a museum (see chapter 7).

Flete, Ermington, Ivybridge PL21 9NZ. Telephone: 075530 308.

Flete is close to the tidal head of the Erme, just 1¼ miles (2 km) downstream from Ermington. A Tudor house was enlarged in about 1795 and changed again not long after with the addition of battlements. In the second half of the nineteenth century the Mildmays employed the architect Richard Norman Shaw to make it their home. Since 1961, the house has been converted into self-contained flats by the Country Houses Association, but the main reception rooms can be viewed. The oak-panelled dining room was the great hall of the early mansion. The large library has an ornate fireplace, and a plaster ceiling in the drawing room is Italian work. The peaceful grounds complement the house, with Italianate and water gardens and mature trees.

Fursdon House, Cadbury, Exeter EX5 5JS. Telephone: 0392 860860.

This home has been lived in by the Fursdon family since about 1259. It is based on a late sixteenth-century house of H-shaped plan around a Great Hall but was greatly altered in 1732 by George Fursdon. He built the entrance in its present position in the centre of the house between two wings. Subsequent additions included the library on the west wing in 1815 and the Ionic colonnade on the front three years later. The dining room has panelled walls and a seventeenth-century table but is separated from the kitchen by 120 feet (36 metres). The library, which is also designed as a ballroom, has a portrait of its builder, George Sydenham Fursdon. The billiard room, formerly a dairy or pantry, has a display of family documents and mementoes. The

museum is in the cobble-floored cellar, game larder and brewhouse and has a good collection of costumes. The finest is a mantua or court dress worn by Elizabeth Fursdon in 1753. The terraced Fox Garden is behind the house, and the rest is parkland.

Garden House, Buckland Monachorum, Yelverton PL20 7LQ. Telephone: 0822 854769.

There are good collections of herbaceous and woody plants in 8 acres (3.2 ha), including a 2 acre (0.8 ha) walled garden said to be among the finest in Britain.

Hartland Abbey, Hartland, near Bideford EX39 6DT. Telephone: 02374 559.

The twelfth-century abbey was dissolved in 1539 and given to William Abbott. Never sold, the property has passed by inheritance to the Stucley family. The main alterations were made in the mid eighteenth century, when the great hall and chapel were demolished and the house built in the Strawberry Hill Gothic style. A century later Sir George Stucley employed Sir George Gilbert Scott to make richly Gothic alterations. His entrance hall and dining room have panelling obtained from the great hall and painted, while the billiard room has a fireplace of Maltese stone brought to Hartland Quay on Stucley's own yacht. The striking Alhambra Corridor was designed by Scott in the style of the Spanish palace. The eighteenth-century servants' hall in the old cloister has an exhibition of documents dating back to the earliest days of the abbey. The house is surrounded by peaceful grounds and shrub gardens in a wooded valley, with paths down to the coast.

Fursdon House, Cadbury.

Killerton House, Broadclyst.

Hemerdon House, Plympton, Plymouth PL7 5BZ. Telephone: 0752 223816 or 337350.

Hemerdon House lies just east of Plympton and is open on thirty days a year in May and August. It was built in the 1790s by George Woollcombe and is still the family home. There are family mementoes from naval and army days and a large collection of paintings and prints including portraits and local scenes by Sir Joshua Reynolds, John Opie and William Bath.

Killerton House and Gardens, Broadclyst, near Exeter EX5 3LE. Telephone: 0392 881345. National Trust.

Killerton, which is the Devon regional office for the National Trust, is 5½ miles (9 km) north-east of Exeter. Sir John Acland purchased the estate in the early seventeenth century. The whole estate of over 6000 acres (2428 ha) was given to the National Trust in 1944 by Sir Richard Acland, the fifteenth Baronet. The village of Broadclyst (see chapter 5) is also part of the estate. The house was built in 1779, although greatly altered in 1898. The furnished rooms open to the public have family portraits and provide a setting for displaying the valuable Paulise de Bush Collection of Costume, which is changed annually. The Music Room has Lydia Acland's organ of 1807. Her tutor was Samuel Wesley, grandson of Charles and an accomplished organist and composer. The Library, with shelves of 1900, contains the Devon library of the Re-

verend Sabine Baring-Gould of Lewtrenchard (see chapter 5). The bedrooms upstairs are named after the smaller Acland estates in Devon, Cornwall and Somerset. The garden has rare trees and shrubs and rises behind the house on the south-facing slope of Dolbury Hill. In the spring the magnolias and rhododendrons are a flame of colour, sheltered under the taller trees. Additional attractions are an ice house and the rustic Bear's Hut. Beyond the hilltop is Killerton Park, with 300 acres (121 ha) of park and woodland. To the east of Killerton, the large Ashclyst Forest with forest walks is part of the estate.

Kirkham House, Kirkham Street, Paignton. English Heritage.

This fifteenth-century town house of red sandstone has been well restored. It may have been the home of a rich merchant or an official at the Bishop's Palace (see chapter 10). There are timber screens on each side of a cobbled entrance passage and the hall reaches to the roof on one side. Displays of furniture range widely in date.

Knightshayes Court and Gardens, Bolham, near Tiverton EX16 7RQ. Telephone: 0884 254665. National Trust.

High on the east side of the Exe valley and approached by a long parkland drive, Knightshayes was built in 1869-74 for Sir John Heathcoat Amory, owner of the great lacemaking factory in Tiverton. The house was designed by William Burges and the stone exterior is complete with imaginative gargoyles. His plans for internal decorations were considered too rich, so these were completed in 1883 by J. D. Crace. Since acquiring the house the National Trust has begun refurnishing and restoring it to its Victorian state. The impressive hall has four columns of black Devon marble supporting a stone balcony and carved corbels with figures of people, animals and birds. A tall bookcase from Burges's London home is here. In the dining room the ceilings have been repainted and wallpaper especially made to one of Crace's designs. The large stone chimney piece in the drawing room was designed by Burges for the hall of Worcester College, Oxford. The gardens around the house are among the finest in Devon. They were first landscaped by Edward Kemp in the late 1870s. Fifty years later Sir Ian Heathcoat Amory cut the Fox and Hounds topiary hedge, but the major changes were made from the 1950s by Sir John and Lady Heathcoat Amory. A Paved Garden and Pool Garden with waterlilies lie within the formal layout with lawns and terraces near the house. Beyond is the large Garden in the Wood, with azaleas, magnolias and rhododendrons. There are other sections, such as a Willow Garden and a Douglas Fir Grove with very tall specimens. In the park at the front of the house is a Turkey oak said to be the largest in Britain.

Marwood Hill Gardens, Marwood, near Barnstaple. Telephone: 0271 42528.

This large garden contains camellias, rhododendrons and rare shrubs, including Australian plants. There are small lakes and alpine, rock, rose and bog gardens.

Oldway Mansion, Paignton. Telephone: 0803 296244, extension 2863. Torbay Borough Council.

The Wigwam was the name given to this mansion which was built in 1875 as the home of Isaac Merritt Singer, founder of the famous sewing-machine company. Alas, he died shortly before its completion. The architect was George Bridgman, whose Rotunda riding and exercising pavilion was completed for Singer two years before. Oldway was much altered by Singer's third son, Paris, in 1904-7. It is very much in the style of the Palace of Versailles, with a Grand Staircase and Gallery with marble floors and walls and richly painted ceilings. The Gallery is a smaller copy of the Hall of Mirrors at Versailles. On the first floor the ballroom has carved and gilt wall panelling. This and the stairs were built on the site of the theatre which Isaac Singer had built in the Wigwam. The second floor is largely unaltered but converted to flats and not open

to the public. Outside, there is an impressive Ionic colonnade along the east facade. The grounds were laid out by the French landscape architect Duchesne. In addition to lawns and trees, there are the formal Italian Garden and the Grotto Gardens with a rock garden and sub-tropical plants, lakes and a waterfall. It was bought in 1946 by Paignton Council and there are now offices here, but the gardens and parts of the mansion are open.

Overbecks, Sharpitor, Salcombe TQ8 8LW. Telephone: 054884 2893. National Trust.

Sharpitor House was built near the mouth of the Salcombe estuary, on the site of an earlier house, in 1913 by G. M. Vereker. It was bought in 1928 by Otto Overbeck, a research chemist and recluse who gathered a large collection about him. When he died in 1937 he left the property to the National Trust for use as a youth hostel, museum and park. The part of the house not used as a hostel forms the museum (see chapter 7), where a room is devoted to Overbeck and his inventions. The terraced garden was begun in the 1900s by Edric Hopkins and continued by Vereker and his wife. The sheltered and mild conditions have been favourable for many plants, such as fuchsias, mimosa, hydrangeas and palms. There are rare trees from Japan and New Zealand, and a giant Himalayan magnolia planted in 1901. The formal statue garden has a bronze by Albert Bruce-Joy, and its flower beds are a blaze of colour in summer. Other features are a sheltered rock dell and the Belvedere, which gives views over the estuary and sea. Sharpitor is a good starting point for cliff walks to Bolt Head (see chapter 2).

Parke, Haytor Road, Bovey Tracey TQ13 9JQ. Telephone: 0626 833909. National Trust.

Parke lies just west of Bovey Tracey and the house is the headquarters of the Dartmoor National Park, where there is an interpretation centre. There are over 200 acres (81 ha) of parkland in the Bovey valley, with woodland walks beside the river and along the course of the Moretonhampstead branch railway (1866 to 1964). The Parke Rare Breeds Farm is also here (see chapter 9).

Powderham Castle, Kenton, Exeter EX6 8JQ. Telephone: 0626 890243.

Powderham Castle is surrounded by a deer park on the west bank of the Exe estuary. Sir Philip Courtenay built the castle in 1390-1420 and it is still lived in by the family of his descendant the Earl of Devon. However, little is visible of the original, for it was badly damaged during the Civil War. The castle today is the result of alterations, first in the eighteenth century when the lower part of the old great hall became the Marble Hall. This has tapestries and a 13 foot (4 metre) high clock made at Totnes in 1740. The staircase hall has rococo plasterwork decorated with animals, birds and flowers. The elegant music room with a domed ceiling was designed by James Wyatt and contains an organ of 1769. Nineteenth-century work includes that of the Devon architect Charles Fowler, such as the medieval-style dining hall with a minstrels' gallery, and the gatehouse and courtyard. The castle grange was converted to the chapel in 1861, retaining its fifteenth-century roof timbers.

Prysten House, Finewell Street, Plymouth. Telephone: 0752 661414.

This wonderful survival behind St Andrew's church is the oldest house in Plymouth. Stone-built in the late fifteenth century, it is believed to be that of a priest or the merchant Thomas Yogge. After becoming a wine store and bacon factory it was restored in 1923, complete with courtyard. Several fine rooms are open, among them the frater and prior's rooms. The Last Supper Room contains a model of Plymouth in 1620, while the Chapter Room has herbal remedies used by Elizabethan voyagers. In the Grammar Room hangs the Plymouth Tapestry, made in 1977-81 and depicting the appointment of the first grammar-school master in 1561. The more ambitious New World Tapestry is being worked on here and elsewhere in Devon. Its 23 panels will tell of the colonisation of America between 1580 and 1643. Near the Door of Unity are buried two American naval officers who died after a battle in the Channel in 1813. A memorial service is held every 30th May, maintaining another Anglo-American link. The nearby

Merchant's House is another good period building and is used as a museum (see chapter 7).

Rosemoor Garden, Great Torrington EX38 7EG. Telephone: 0805 24067.

Just south-east of Great Torrington, in the wooded Torridge valley, with over 8 acres (3.2 ha) of varied gardens, with rhododendrons, roses, shrubs and trees, the garden was begun in 1959 by Lady Anne Palmer, who donated it to the Royal Horticultural Society. It is being enlarged to 40 acres (16.2 ha) with a visitor centre added in 1989.

St Nicholas Priory, The Mint, off Fore Street, Exeter. Telephone: 0392 265858. Exeter Museums Service.

A Benedictine priory was founded here in 1070 by monks from Battle Abbey, but most was demolished after the Dissolution. The guest wing survived and became the home of the Mallett family, who added plaster ceilings. The fifteenth-century guest hall and kitchen can be viewed as well as a fine Norman undercroft. A small garden outside is on the site of the priory church.

Saltram House, Plympton, Plymouth PL7 3OH. Telephone: 0752 336546. National Trust.

This is a superb George II mansion, well proportioned with two wings and with its original contents. Towards the end of the eighteenth century John Parker improved an elegant house created by his mother. There are two rooms in the east wing by Robert Adam, the large Drawing Room with a painted ceiling and Axminster carpet to his

Prysten House, Plymouth.

47

Saltram House, Plympton.

design and the Dining Room. During a re-arrangement the Dining Room was formed from the old library, while the books were put in what was once called the Eating Room. Among the fine furniture is a four-poster bed by Thomas Chippendale in the Chinese Chippendale Room. Paintings by the locally born artist Sir Joshua Reynolds are well represented, including many of the Parker family. The kitchen and stables are also worth viewing. The garden has an orangery, and the landscaped park descends to the banks of the tidal Plym estuary.

Sand, Sidbury, Sidmouth EX10 0QN. Telephone: 03957 230.

Once known as Sand Barton, the house stands in attractive country just off the Sid valley. It is said that Catherine of Aragon stayed here on her journey from Plymouth to London to marry Prince Arthur, brother of Henry VIII. Owned by the Huyshe family since 1560, the earlier manor house was incorporated when it was substantially rebuilt by Rowland Huyshe in 1592-4. By coincidence it was repaired in 1908-9 by another Rowland. Inside the porch are the passage, oak screen and Great Hall. The library with a fifteenth-century fireplace is part of the older building. The former kitchen is now a sitting room. Sand Lodge is a restored longhouse, probably of the fifteenth century.

Tapeley Park, Instow, Bideford EX39 4NT. Telephone: 0271 860528.

This large William and Mary house over-looks the Taw-Torridge estuary just south of Instow. In 1855 William Langham Christie of Glyndebourne, Sussex, married into the Cleveland family, who had owned the house since 1702. He altered the facade, but his daughter-in-law Lady Rosamond made the best improvements, using the architect John Belcher. For example, a plaster ceiling was added to the dining room and a room was built in 1802 by John Clevland, who was Member of Parliament for Barnstaple for nearly forty years. Fine furniture includes pieces by William Morris and ebony tables once the property of Warren Hastings, who had an eventful career with the East India Company. Outside the house, the beautiful terraced Italian Garden has statues and a pool. There are pavilions, an ice house and a shell house. The grounds also include a walled kitchen garden, woodland lake and picnic areas.

Torre Abbey, King's Drive, Torquay. Telephone: 0803 23593. Torbay Borough Council.

Founded here near the shore of Torbay in 1196, Torre Abbey had become the Premonstratensian order's richest monastery at the Dissolution in 1539. Part became the home of the Ridgeway family after 1598, but the major alterations were made in the first part of the eighteenth century by the Carys. In 1930 the house was sold to Torquay (now Torbay) Borough Council. The Torbay mayor has a suite of rooms here and the rest is open to the public as the council's museum and art gallery (see chapter 7). Of survivals from the abbey, the Mohun Gateway of 1330 is impressive, with red sandstone arches and the arms of the de Mohuns carved on the exterior. The Abbot's Tower is in the west range where the abbot's apartments and guest hall remain, but the upper part was converted into a house. The chapter-house wall and doorway are well preserved but the central tower has collapsed. Excavations have revealed further evidence of the chancel and other buildings. The tithe barn dates from the beginning of the abbey and is now called the Spanish Barn as prisoners from the Armada were held here in 1588.

The lower part of the monks' refectory became the entrance hall in the south range of the new house. One room here was used by Earl St Vincent when the Channel Fleet was based at Torbay in 1801. The main living rooms are on the first floor and an oak staircase is the main feature to survive from the Ridgeways' early Jacobean house. The dining room was reconstructed by the Carys soon after 1662. This Catholic family built a secret chapel in the roof space above. This was abandoned and a vaulted ceiling inserted when the present chapel was built out of the monastery's old guest hall in 1779. Other rooms include a charming bedroom restored to its late Victorian appearance, with reproduction William Morris wallpaper. The walls of the clock-tower are early thirteenth-century, one room being Colonel Cary's study in about 1908. There are kitchens in the south-west wing and the Torre Abbey Room traces the history of the abbey, featuring a model of it as it was in 1530. Behind the house and abbey ruins are attractive formal gardens, laid out since council ownership, and a 1939 palm house, which was rebuilt in 1969.

Ugbrooke Park, Chudleigh TQ13 0AD. Telephone: 0626 852179.

Built upon earlier foundations, the Tudor house at Ugbrooke came into the Clifford family in the sixteenth century at the marriage of Sir Piers Courtenay's daughter Ann to Anthony Clifford. The fourth Lord Clifford commissioned Robert Adam to redesign the house and the result was a new building with towers and battlements. The Catholic chapel of 1673 was refurbished by Adam in the Italian style. The house is lived in and has fine furniture and paintings. The drawing room has portraits of Charles II and his wife. The seventh Lord Clifford married the daughter of Cardinal Weld, a widower who took holy orders. The Cardinal's Bedroom with its four-poster bed was used by him on visits. A painting shows him with the Pope. The Tapestry Room has good seventeenth-century Mortlake tapestries. Items of family interest are exhibited elsewhere. 'Capability' Brown landscaped the park, planting trees and creating lakes and a waterfall. Attractions for visitors include walks, ornamental birds and wildfowl, an aviary and facilities for angling.

Ugbrooke Park, Chudleigh.

7
Museums and art galleries

APPLEDORE
North Devon Maritime Museum, Odun House, Odun Road, Appledore. Telephone: 02372 79138.

The museum is in the former residence of mariners, merchants and shipowners and tells the story of the district's interesting maritime history. Models, photographs, tools and other artefacts explain local shipbuilding, shipowning and trading, fishing, lifesaving and the gravel barges of the estuary. A photographic record shows training with landing craft in and around the estuary and sands during the Second World War. In contrast one room has a reconstructed Victorian kitchen.

ASHBURTON
Ashburton Museum, 1 West Street, Ashburton TQ13 7AB. Telephone: 0364 53278.

Displays on three floors have items of local interest including Elizabethan documents, Ashburton worthies and events, minerals, locally made bottles and domestic items. In

St Anne's Chapel, Barnstaple.

contrast the top floor contains the Paul Endacott Bequest, a collection of North American Indian artefacts. There is also a reading room available for research.

AXMINSTER
Axminster Museum, The Old Courthouse, Church Street, Axminster. Telephone: 0297 34146.

Local archaeology includes flints, Roman tiles and tiles from the old Cistercian Newenham Abbey. There is a growing collection of domestic and agricultural implements and photographs, and a display on the Axminster carpet industry from its beginnings in 1755. Of interest are the christening gloves of John Churchill, the first Duke of Marlborough, who was born at nearby Ashe House in 1650.

BARNSTAPLE
Lynton and Barnstaple Railway Museum, The Signal Box, Old Town Station, Castle Street, Barnstaple EX31 1DR.

There are interesting relics and photographs in this tiny museum in the old signal box at the disused Barnstaple Town Station, now a restaurant. This famous narrow-gauge railway (see chapter 8) had its terminus here, where passengers transferred to and from the railway to Ilfracombe.

Museum of North Devon, North Devon Athenaeum, The Square, Barnstaple EX32 8LN. Telephone: 0271 46747.

The refurbished museum covers the archaeology, natural history, militaria and pottery industry of the north Devon region. An unusual display is the Victorian Fernery, with growing British ferns illustrating the Victorian fern craze.

St Anne's Chapel and Old Grammar School Museum, St Peter's Churchyard, High Street, Barnstaple.

The thirteenth-century chapel became a grammar school from the sixteenth century until 1910. It contains a recreated schoolroom with oak furniture of the late seventeenth century, when the poet John Gay was a pupil here. The history of schooling is also described.

BIDEFORD
Burton Art Gallery, Kingsley Road, Bideford. Telephone: 02372 76711, extension 315.

Thomas Burton and Hubert Coop created this gallery around their collections in 1951. There are paintings by Coop himself and

Fairlynch Arts Centre and Museum, Budleigh Salterton.

portraits by Sir Joshua Reynolds and John Opie. Pottery includes Bideford harvest jugs of the late eighteenth century, and there are items of silver and pewter. Bone model ships are a feature, made by French prisoners during the Napoleonic Wars, for there was a prison camp at Bideford. The gallery has changing exhibitions, and there are plans for expansion to form a museum of the Bideford district.

BRAUNTON
Braunton and District Museum, Church House, Church Street, Braunton.

The museum is in the old Church House, beside St Brannock's church at the north end of the town. Displays concern the life and work of the area in farming and seafaring.

BRIXHAM
British Fisheries Museum, The Old Market House, The Quay, Brixham. Telephone: 08045 2861.

The museum takes the whole of the top floor of the Old Market House and appropriately looks out over Brixham's fishing harbour. The history of national inshore and distant trawling — sail, steam and diesel — is well displayed through photographs, drawings and some models. Important regions and fishing types include Brixham and Cornwall.

Brixham Museum, incorporating **HM Coastguard National Museum**, Bolton Cross, Brixham. Telephone: 08045 6267.

Models of Brixham sailing trawlers are part of an exhibition on this famous local industry. Boatbuilding was another important trade and the museum has an outstanding collection of traditional boatbuilding tools. A famous wooden vessel built at Brixham was the replica *Mayflower II*, which repeated the voyage across the Atlantic in 1957. Among the earliest land-based exhibits are a bronze age skeleton and pottery, attesting the suitability of this site for settlement. There are displays of costumes and handicrafts, such as pillow lace made by women from the seventeenth century onwards. Victorian Brixham also features. Another link with the sea is embroidered pictures made by seamen from the port. The HM Coastguard National Museum relates the history of the service, set up in 1822 to counter smuggling. A reconstructed operations room of the nineteenth century contrasts with displays of the modern service, which coordinates search and rescue operations around the whole of Britain.

BUDLEIGH SALTERTON
Fairlynch Arts Centre and Museum, Budleigh Salterton. Telephone: 03954 2666.

This thatched museum close to the sea front

contains exhibits on local history, natural history, costumes, lacemaking (demonstrated at times) and a smugglers' cellar. There are changing exhibitions in the art gallery.

CHITTLEHAMPTON
Cobbaton Combat Vehicles Museum, Cobbaton, near Chittlehampton, Umberleigh EX37 9SD. Telephone: 07694 414.

This collection of over thirty vehicles, mainly British and Canadian of the Second World War period, includes a 44-ton Churchill tank, guns, armoured cars and carriers. There is also an American Sherman tank and a Patton M47, which was developed between the Korean and Vietnam wars. The civilian aspect of wartime is shown in a Home Front section, with many small period items such as photographs, newspapers and a baby's gas-mask.

COMBE MARTIN
Combe Martin Motor Cycle Collection, Cross Street, Combe Martin EX34 0DH. Telephone: 027188 2346.

The collection is in a small former garage near the sea-front car park and includes British motorcycles of all periods. There are signs, petrol pumps and other old garage items.

CROYDE
Croyde Gem, Rock and Shell Museum, 10 Hobbs Hill, Croyde, Braunton. Telephone: 0271 890407.

This is a beautiful display of gems, minerals, rocks and shells from all over the world. There are large and colourful crystals and some rare radio-active minerals. Gemstones and minerals are cut and polished on the premises, for display and jewellery.

DARTMOUTH
Dartmouth Museum, The Butterwalk, Duke Street, Dartmouth TQ6 9PZ. Telephone: 08043 2923.

The museum is on the first floor of the historic Butterwalk, one of the finest seventeenth-century merchant's houses in Devon, reconstructed after enemy bomb damage in 1943. There is a maritime flavour everywhere, with models, paintings and photographs relating to Dartmouth and the estuary. There are mementoes of Thomas Newcomen, a Dartmouth ironmonger who invented the atmospheric beam engine later developed by Boulton and Watt. A restored engine is preserved nearby (see chapter 8). The rooms themselves are of interest, with panelled walls and decorative plaster ceilings. Charles II is said to have been entertained in the King's Room. The building has a pole staircase, probably around a ship's mast, with irregular stairs designed to trip up night-time intruders.

Henley Museum, Anzac Street, Dartmouth. Dartmouth Town Council.

This museum contains a collection of the Victorian everyday possessions of William Henley (1860-1919), a Dartmouth sage. There are paintings, photographs, shells, fossils, rare books, a microscope and slides, and a recon-

Dartmouth Museum is in the historic Butterwalk.

The Butts Ferry crosses the Exe, linking Exeter Maritime Museum with the city's quay area.

struction of Henley's own living room.

DAWLISH
Dawlish Museum, Knowle House, Barton Terrace, Dawlish.

This is a museum of local history, with old photographs, original drawings of the South Devon Railway and painted posters from the station waiting room. Reconstructed rooms are a feature, such as a Victorian bedroom, kitchen, parlour and nursery. Military exhibits include a nostalgic collection of ration books and coupons. There are costume dolls, a costume gallery and a display of Honiton lace.

EAST BUDLEIGH
James Countryside Museum, Bicton Park, East Budleigh, Budleigh Salterton. Telephone: 0395 68465.

A good display of farming equipment of all types is one part of the many attractions at Bicton Park (see chapter 6), collected by N. D. G. James, former land agent to the Clinton Estates. Included are traction engines, farm machinery and implements, cidermaking equipment and working models.

EXETER
Devonshire Regiment Museum, Wyvern Barracks, Exeter EX2 6AE. Telephone: 0392 218178.

First raised in 1685 as the Duke of

Beaufort's Musketeers, the regiment was known as the Devonshires from 1881 to 1958, when it was amalgamated with the Dorsets. The museum has uniforms, medals, photographs and illustrations of campaigns. The Devonshires were active at the siege of Ladysmith and an unusual Boer War memento is an ostrich egg from Kruger's farm. The Second Battalion was awarded the French *Croix de Guerre* for action at Bois de Buttes in 1918, when there were 551 casualties.

Exeter Maritime Museum, The Haven, Exeter EX2 8DT. Telephone: 0392 58075.

The International Sailing Craft Association's museum contains a very large collection of worldwide craft, many afloat in Exeter Canal Haven and others indoors in the refurbished Victorian warehouses. Visitors are encouraged to touch and explore the boats and working equipment such as a windlass, capstan and pump. Amongst the largest of the floating collection are a magnificent pearling dhow from Bahrain, a genuine Chinese junk and a beautifully painted Portuguese lighter. There are eight colourful Indonesian boats, the largest of which can be boarded in the Haven. Among the smaller boats is a fascinating rowing collection: African dugouts, South American reed boats and proas from the South Seas. British vessels include the Bedford Lifeboat and the TSW *Shamrock*, an oyster smack from Colchester. Two contrasting steam vessels in working order are the curious *Bertha*, Brunel's dredger of 1844, and the former Fowey tug *St Canute*, built in Scandinavia in 1931. Most of the museum is in and around the Canal Haven, but there is more at Exeter Quay, reached by the historic Butts Ferry.

Rougemont House Museum of Costume and Lace, Castle Street, Exeter. Telephone: 0392 265858.

John Patch, an Exeter surgeon, built the house in the 1770s close to the gatehouse of Rougemont Castle and created a landscaped garden from the moat. Altered to the Regency style in 1810 and purchased by the City Council in 1911, it is now the setting for this museum, opened in 1987. The large and changing collection of costumes dates from the 1740s to the present day. There are displays of very fine Honiton lace and more from other parts of the world, some worn by royalty. In addition, there are temporary exhibitions and demonstrations.

Royal Albert Memorial Museum, Queen Street, Exeter EX4 3RX. Telephone: 0392 265858.

This impressive building opened in 1868 contains art galleries with works by Devon artists as well as visiting exhibitions. Pottery, glass and Exeter silver are also on show. The large ethnography section has artefacts from the North American Indians, the Amazon, West Africa, Australia and the Pacific islands. Worldwide and Devon natural history is displayed, and the archaeology gallery explains Devon's past and includes a model of the Roman legionary bath house in Exeter.

Spacex Gallery, 45 Preston Street, Exeter. Telephone: 0392 31786.

This gallery holds changing exhibitions of contemporary art.

EXMOUTH
Country Life Museum, Sandy Bay, Exmouth EX8 5BU. Telephone: 0395 274533.

This is a large complex, mostly under cover. There are working machines and models. In the transport section are vintage cars, motorcycles, fire engines and stationary engines, as well as steam engines, agricultural tractors and a model railway engine. A furnished Victorian cottage, shop and toyroom are among the exhibits. Crafts are demonstrated. The animal collection has llamas, wallabies, Highland cattle, Shire horses, donkeys and many farmyard animals and birds. There is a large deer park, with red, fallow and sika deer, through which visitors ride on a tractor train.

Exmouth Museum, Sheppards Row, off Exeter Road, Exmouth.

The museum is housed in former council stables. A major new display is mounted every season with the object of establishing continued interest, and smaller displays are periodically presented, either with a local or national flavour. These are normally on show for a limited period only.

GREAT TORRINGTON
Torrington Museum, Town Hall, High Street, Great Torrington EX38 8HN. Telephone: 0805 24324.

Displays of local artefacts include dairy, domestic and pharmaceutical equipment and Torrington giftware. Specially featured are the robes and coronets of the Earl and Countess Orford: the Earl's were worn for the coronation of George V and Queen Mary in 1911 and those of the Countess at the coronation of George VI and Queen Elizabeth in 1937.

HARTLAND QUAY
Hartland Quay Museum, Hartland Quay, near Bideford EX39 6DU. Telephone: 028883 353.

The museum is beside the Hartland Quay Hotel down by the shore. Aided by models, pictures and photographs, exhibits explain the history of the coastal shipping trade to the old quay which was destroyed by storms in the nineteenth century. A special shipwreck room records wrecks and lifesaving from the seventeenth century to the present day. The Hartland Point lighthouse is also represented, as well as the fauna, flora and geology of the cliffs and shore.

HOLSWORTHY
Holsworthy Museum, The Manor Offices, Holsworthy. Telephone: 0409 253336.

This good little museum contains agricultural and domestic implements, china and other items of local interest.

HONITON
Allhallows Museum, High Street, Honiton EX14 8PE. Telephone: 0404 3106.

The museum is next to St Paul's church and the main gallery is in the thirteenth-century chancel of Allhallows Chapel, which became a schoolroom. There is material from prehistory to the present relating to the local history of Honiton. One gallery is devoted to a large display of the world-famous Honiton lace, and lacemaking demonstrations are given daily in the tourist season.

ILFRACOMBE
Ilfracombe Museum, Wilder Road, Ilfracombe EX34 8AF. Telephone: 0271 63541.

In a building of 1885, the museum contains over twenty thousand exhibits of natural history, Victoriana, war memorabilia, paintings, prints and photographs of old Ilfracombe. There is also a brass-rubbing centre.

INSTOW
Porcupines Toy Museum and Bookroom, Myrtle Cottage, Kiln Close Lane, Instow. Telephone: 0271 861158.

A small museum with a bookroom is packed with mainly Victorian and Edwardian period dolls, dolls' houses and toys.

KINGSBRIDGE
Cookworthy Museum, The Old Grammar School, 108 Fore Street, Kingsbridge TQ7 1AW. Telephone: 0548 3235.

The museum is named after William Cookworthy (1705-80) of Kingsbridge, who became a Plymouth chemist and discovered china clay in Cornwall. This enabled porcelain to be made and led to the creation of one of the largest industries in the South-west. It is likely that he came here as a boy, for the building is the grammar school founded by Thomas Crispin in 1670. The main room retains a high canopied schoolmaster's chair at one end and wood panelling carved with the names of pupils over the years. The Crispin Room illustrates the history of the school. As well as old photographs of Kingsbridge there are exhibitions on the landscape, natural history, railways, turnpikes and industries, all relating to the Kingsbridge area. A pharmacy is rich in detail, reconstructed by the Park Pharmacy Trust. The farm gallery contains a large cider press and horse-powered apple crusher with granite rollers.

LYNTON
Lyn and Exmoor Museum, Market Street, Lynton EX35 6DQ.

Dating from the early eighteenth century, this is one of the oldest houses in the district. It has a slate slab roof and the restored Exmoor kitchen has its original lime-ash floor. Exhibits include old Exmoor arts and crafts, and farming implements for uses as varied as turf-cutting, thatching and poaching. There is a maritime display from the days of sail, also featuring the lifeboat service, for the Lynmouth lifeboat took part in a famous rescue in 1899 when it was hauled overland to be launched at Porlock Weir in Somerset.

OKEHAMPTON
Museum of Dartmoor Life, The Dartmoor Centre, West Street, Okehampton EX20 1HQ. Telephone: 0837 53020.

The museum is in a former mill and store of 1811 and its three floors and extension have displays on geology, archaeology and folk life. Displays of Dartmoor industries include mining, quarrying, china clay, glass manufacturing

and even icemaking. A wheelwright's shop and cider press represent rural crafts. Farming transport exhibits include wagons and a vintage tractor. The courtyard has craft shops, tea rooms and a National Park information centre.

OTTERTON
Otterton Mill and Gallery, Otterton, near Budleigh Salterton EX9 7HG. Telephone: 0395 68521 and 68031.

The restored watermill worked by the river Otter produces wholemeal flour and also contains a mill museum which explains its workings. The Otterton Mill Gallery has a changing programme of art exhibitions and occasional concerts. Craft workshops include pottery, wood turning, printing, patchwork and quilting. The mill is at the bottom of an attractive village of white thatched cottages with an intermittent stream between Fore Street and the pavement.

PLYMOUTH
Merchant's House, 33 St Andrews Street, Plymouth. Telephone: 0752 264878.

The four floors of this sixteenth-century town house are devoted to a museum of Plymouth's history, told through the themes of Tinker, Tailor, Soldier, Sailor, Rich Man, Poor Man, Apothecary, Thief. These include displays on the Eddystone lighthouse, Plymouth defences and the Blitz of the Second World War. Most memorable is the superbly reconstructed Park's pharmacy of the mid nineteenth century.

Plymouth City Museum and Art Gallery, Drake Circus, Plymouth PL4 8AJ. Telephone: 0752 264878.

There is an impressive facade to the city art gallery, museum and library, built in 1907-10. The art gallery has works by the South-west painters Stanhope Forbes and C. Napier Hemy, and the Cottonian Collection has portraits by Sir Joshua Reynolds, who came from Plympton, including one of himself. Among the ceramics is Plymouth porcelain of 1768-70 by William Cookworthy (see Cookworthy Museum, Kingsbridge, above). The natural history and geology of the Plymouth district are also displayed.

SALCOMBE
Overbecks Museum, Sharpitor, Salcombe TQ8 8LW. Telephone: 054884 2893.

Overbecks is best known for its garden left to the National Trust by Otto Overbeck in 1937 (see chapter 6). The early twentieth-century house, now mostly a youth hostel, also contains a museum. Of local maritime interest there are shipwrights' tools and paintings and photographs of shipping and shipwrecks. The latter include the beautiful four-masted barque

Herzogin Cecile, wrecked at Soar Mill Cove in 1936. In contrast, there are dolls and dolls' houses and a collection of animals, birds, eggs and shells. The Overbeck Room contains Overbeck's rejuvenator, a life regenerator of 'improved' type.

Salcombe Museum of Maritime and Local History, Cook's Boat Store, Custom House Quay, Salcombe.

The museum is located in a boat store on the quay during the summer months. It records Salcombe's maritime history, especially the nineteenth century, when fast schooners worked the citrus fruit trade with Spain and the Azores, and the Newfoundland fish trade. There are also shipbuilding, wreck and rescue sections, and a record of the American activities at Salcombe during the Second World War.

SIDMOUTH
Sidmouth Museum, Hope Cottage, Church Street, Sidmouth EX10 8LY. Telephone: 0395 516139.

The museum is provided by the Sid Vale Association, founded in 1846 and the first civic

One of the waterwheels at the Finch Foundry Museum, Sticklepath.

society in Britain. A good collection of prints records Sidmouth in the early nineteenth century, but outstanding is the Long Picture by Hubert Cornish, some 8 feet (2.4 metres) long, depicting the whole of Sidmouth sea-front in about 1814. A large exhibit is a Columbian press, which worked for a local printer for 139 years. Local geology is explained and the archaeological collection has finds from the Holcombe Roman villa site, including a copy of a bronze mirror of iron age date. There is a small display about Peter Orlando Hutchinson, author, artist, historian and diarist of Sidmouth, who built the Chancel, incorporating the old chancel from Sidmouth's church and the south transept from Awliscombe (chapter 10). Other displays cover famous local people, costumes, tools, Victoriana and photographs of events over the last hundred years. There are exhibitions and demonstrations of lace and corn-dolly making from time to time.

Vintage Toy and Train Museum, Field's Department Store, Market Place, Sidmouth EX10 8LU. Telephone: 0395 515124, extension 34.

The museum contains toys from 1925 to 1975, such as tinplate trains and die-cast toys, constructional sets, jigsaws, lead soldier figures and books.

SOUTH MOLTON
South Molton Museum, Guildhall, Broad Street, South Molton. Telephone: 07695 2951.

This was voted the *Illustrated London News* Best Small Museum for 1987. Larger items are Newsham's fire engine of 1736, used until 1886, when replaced by the Merryweather machine also on display. A small archaeological collection includes a fine neolithic greenstone axe from Filleigh. North Devon mining is represented by geological specimens, maps and diagrams. There are old photographs of South Molton, and pride of place is given to the borough charters granted by Elizabeth I (1590) and Charles II (1684). Some exhibits are changed to show more of the museum's collection, and there are also art exhibitions.

STICKLEPATH
Finch Foundry Museum, Sticklepath, Okehampton. Telephone: 0837 840286.

Sticklepath is best known for the Finch family's foundry (see chapter 8), but there are also museum galleries displaying tools made or used at the foundry. The historical development of water-powered machinery is shown as well as a small display on local geology.

TAVISTOCK
Tavistock Museum, Drake Road, Tavistock.

The museum was begun in late 1986 and has

a growing collection of items and photographs mainly reflecting the district in the nineteenth century, with mining and agriculture especially represented. Local minerals, early prints of Tavistock Abbey and the old town stocks are on display. There is a small section on Sir Francis Drake, who was born at nearby Crowndale.

TEIGNMOUTH
Teignmouth Museum, 26 French Street, Teignmouth.

Here are finds from a shipwreck discovered just offshore at Church Rocks in 1975, including part of a gun carriage, a bronze saker cannon and a bronze-barrelled breach-loading swivel gun of the late sixteenth century. There are also displays of other shipwrecks and the Teignmouth lifeboat. The port is represented too, especially the important ball-clay trade. A toll board from the Shaldon Bridge was removed when tolls were abolished in 1948. There are also household items, Victoriana, paintings and prints. A railway section has staff uniforms and a piece of atmospheric pipe from Brunel's railway (see chapter 8).

TIVERTON
Tiverton Museum, The Old School, St Andrew Street, Tiverton. Telephone: 0884 256295.

This large museum is housed in a former school and packed with exhibits of all kinds, many of local interest. There is a large agricultural section with tools and equipment, including cidermaking. A collection of man traps has one 'humane' type. A special gallery is devoted to lace and lacemaking machinery. John Heathcoat's factory at Tiverton has made lace for royal wedding veils, and wartime work included making parachutes and barrage balloons as well as aircraft and tank parts. The wagon gallery has a good collection, and an unusual three-wheeled 'Bampton barrow' used for carrying earth or stone in the district. There is also a nineteenth-century horse-wheel which worked farm machinery. Pride of place in the railway exhibition goes to the Tivvy Bumper, a Great Western Railway tank locomotive which served on the Exe valley and Culm valley lines, closed to passenger traffic in 1963. Outside the museum there are two large waterwheels of local manufacture.

TOPSHAM
Topsham Museum, Holman House, 25 The Strand, Topsham EX3 0AX. Telephone: 0392 873251.

The museum is in a seventeenth-century merchant's house, refurbished in 1739. The rooms have been arranged for a shipmaster's family of the period. A sail loft, added in 1858, now displays the maritime and social history of Topsham, then a trading and shipbuilding port

on the Exe. Items include shipwrights' tools and models, pictures and photographs of Topsham-built vessels. The natural history and birds of the Exe estuary are also displayed.

TORQUAY
Bygones, Fore Street, St Marychurch, Torquay TQ1 4PR. Telephone: 0803 36108.

There is a reconstructed Victorian street with shops, period display rooms, a forge and public house. The largest exhibit is a steam locomotive of 1929 from Falmouth docks. On a smaller scale, there are a model railway layout, an illuminated grotto and a collection of medals and militaria.

Torquay Museum, 529 Babbacombe Road, Torquay TQ1 1HG. Telephone: 0803 23975.

The Torquay Natural History Society had been founded for thirty years when their fine museum building was opened in 1875. The Holden Gallery explains the geology of south Devon and the natural history includes finds from Kents Cavern (chapter 9), such as bones of hyena, cave lions, mammoths and woolly rhinoceros. Kents Cavern also gave up the oldest modern human bone in Britain, part of a woman's jawbone 30,900 years old. This is displayed in the new Archaeology Gallery, where there are also hand axes perhaps half a million years old, harpoons and other palaeolithic artefacts. William Pengelly was one of the pioneer cave excavators and his study has been recreated here. The archaeology of south Devon also includes mesolithic and neolithic flints and an important bronze duck, bird and stag from the iron age camp at Milber Down near Newton Abbot. There are Roman, Saxon and medieval finds, the last including tiles from Torre Abbey (chapters 6 and 7). Elsewhere in the museum, the Leach Gallery has pictorial records of south Devon and Torquay over 150 years. There are farming tools, household items and a reconstructed lady's workroom. Local industries displayed include marble, represented by a table top with forty varieties of local marbles. Watcombe terracotta was important at St Marychurch in the second half of the nineteenth century.

Torre Abbey Museum and Art Gallery, The Kings Drive, Torquay TQ2 5JX. Telephone: 0803 293593.

The house, abbey and gardens are described in chapter 6, but the house contains a good collection of art works. The main galleries display paintings, silver, English glass and the locally made Torquay and Watcombe terracotta wares. Among the paintings and drawings are works by Sir Edward Burne-Jones and engravings by William Blake. There are sculptures and a programme of exhibitions.

The museum of the Torquay Natural History Society dates from 1875.

TOTNES

British Photographic Museum, Bowden House, Totnes TQ9 7PW.

This award-winning museum in the grounds of Bowden House (chapter 6) tells the history of photography, with many still and movie cameras of all sizes and ages on show. There are changing exhibitions of photographs, a display of cartoon animation, a Victorian studio, an Edwardian darkroom and replica shops.

Devonshire Collection of Period Costume, Bogan House, 43 High Street, Totnes TQ9 6DS. Telephone: 0803 862423.

A selection of costumes and accessories ranging from 1750 to the present day is displayed in themes rather than periods, in exhibitions which are changed annually.

Totnes Elizabethan Museum, 70 Fore Street, Totnes. Telephone: 0803 863821.

Built about 1575, this is a fine architectural example of a rich merchant's house of the period, altered about 1620 with a great pole incorporated in the staircase. Six principal rooms are connected by a gallery to a kitchen block, cobbled courtyard and Elizabethan herb garden. There is a permanent exhibition on Charles Babbage (1791-1871), father of the computer, who attended the local King Edward VI Grammar School. His inventions included the difference and analytical engines, the 'cowcatcher' for trains, the occulting light for night signalling and the ophthalmoscope for eye treatment. A small display commemorates another of the town's famous sons, William John Wills (1834-61), second-in-command of the ill-fated Burke and Wills expedition in Australia in 1860-1. Wills and others perished on the return journey. Also on display are a Victorian nursery and shop, local pottery from the sixteenth and seventeenth centuries, a tenth-century Totnes-minted silver coin, the eleventh-century ivory seal of a Norman French lord, period costumes and much else.

Totnes Motor Museum, Steamer Quay, Totnes TQ9 5AL. Telephone: 0803 862777.

The collection includes vintage, sports and racing cars of famous makes, all kept in perfect running order. Other types range from the Austin 7 to the Amphicar, which can cross water. There are also old instruments, books, motorcycles and a 1930s garage display.

8
Industrial archaeology

The heritage of the industrial past in Devon is largely a rural one and includes good examples of mills (corn and textile), mines, quarries and limekilns, as well as railways and canals. It is difficult to believe that the scenic Tamar valley in west Devon was a centre of industry in the nineteenth century. Dartmoor, already rich in prehistoric archaeology, also has industrial relics of tin mining, granite working, gunpowder mills, tramways and leats. Some mills and railways are included in chapter 9, and a selection of the other sites is given here.

Beer Quarry Caves, Quarry Lane, Beer, Seaton EX12 3DZ. Telephone: 0297 80282 or 20986.

In these superb underground workings Beer stone, a white freestone occurring near the base of the Middle Chalk, much prized for carving in Devon churches, notably Exeter Cathedral, was mined. The stone has been worked underground since Roman times and transported nationwide, and the extensive chambers are supported by pillars of uncut stone, some vaulted. Guides show how the stone was extracted and point out inscriptions of quarry workers on the walls. The maze of workings was used by smugglers in the nineteenth century.

Birch Tor and Vitifer Mine, Dartmoor. Just east of the Warren House Inn on the B3212 from Moretonhampstead and reached by footpath.

This major Dartmoor tin mine was worked intermittently from the mid eighteenth century until 1926, though there were probably medieval workings in the valley. There are extensive areas of surface and underground workings with remains of mine buildings, the mine captain's house, miners' house, carpenter's shop and so on. A leat brought water from the East Dart over 7 miles (11.2 km) away. The deep openworks which cross Headland Warren can be seen from Grimspound (see chapter 3).

Broadclyst windmill tower, Broadclyst, near Exeter (SX 991966).

The windmill worked from 1786 to 1815 and is unusual in that the tower was converted into housing after a disastrous fire in Broadclyst in 1870. It is the best remaining windmill tower in Devon and can be seen just east of the village. There are other towers in the county, notably around the south end of Torbay.

Brunel Atmospheric Railway, The Old Pumping House, Starcross, Exeter EX6 8PR. Telephone: 0626 890000.

The old pumping station was built in 1845 for Brunel's atmospheric railway experiment along the South Devon Railway between Exeter and Newton Abbot. There are guided tours, audio-visual shows and a working atmospheric railway to explain the operation of this unusual type of transport. Visitors can view the old boiler houses and engine room, which housed two steam engines for exhausting the air from the pipes of the railway system. Visitors can also climb the tower, which gives good views. The original decorated chimney was built 50 feet (15 metres) higher. The building, in coarse red conglomerate with pale limestone arches, stands in a narrow site between the main road through Starcross, with its few humble Georgian houses, and the railway line, beyond which is the Exe estuary. A ferry crosses from near the station to Exmouth in summer.

Cann Quarry and Canal, near Plymouth.

A canal of 2 miles (3.2 km) was built in 1829 by the Earl of Morley from the Cann slate quarry in the Plym valley to a tramway at Marsh Mills. Within six years the tramway was extended alongside the canal and its stone sleeper blocks can still be seen. The flooded quarry (SX 524596) is beside the Plym and a viaduct of the old Tavistock branch railway in the Plym Bridge Woods (see chapter 2). Another important source of slate in west Devon was Mill Hill near Tavistock, which is still at work.

Cherry Brook Powder Mills, near Two Bridges, Dartmoor.

A gunpowder mill worked at this isolated spot from 1844 until the 1890s. The old mills and two chimneys can be seen just north of the B3212 between Two Bridges and Postbridge. There is also a mortar which was used for testing the powder. A row of workers' cottages has been restored and contains a forge (see chapter 9).

Coldharbour Mill, Uffculme, Cullompton EX15 3EE. Telephone: 0884 40960.

At this working woollen mill and museum in a pleasant setting at the west end of Uffculme village textiles have been produced since 1797. Visitors can see carding, spinning and weaving machinery, a reconstructed weavers' workshop and dye room. There are an 18 foot (5.5 metre) diameter waterwheel and a 1910 steam engine together with craft workshops, an audio-visual presentation, mill shop, gardens and restaurant.

Coldharbour Mill, Uffculme.

Devonport Dockyard, Devonport.

The royal dockyard was founded in 1691 and now covers 2 miles (3.2 km) of the Hamoaze shore, its two sites separated by the Torpoint chain ferry. It was expanded many times, notably with the Keyham steam yard in the 1850s and major works at the beginning of the twentieth century. The process of modernisation continues today, but several structures and buildings of historical interest remain within the complex. Guided tours are available to some parts. An impressive piece of architecture stands across Stonehouse Creek: the Royal William Victualling Yard, built by John Rennie in 1826-35. The grand entrance gateway is in granite and has carved ox heads, the whole surmounted by a statue of William IV. The future of the yard is uncertain but it is likely to be preserved in some form. The group of buildings and quays can be viewed from the Cremyll ferry.

Exeter Canal, Exeter.

Built in the 1560s, and improved twice just over a century later, the Exeter Canal is the oldest ship canal in Britain, taking shipping into the heart of the city. The last improvement was in 1824 by James Green, who extended the canal southwards to Turf Lock to gain better access from the estuary. He also built the city basin, which is surrounded by period warehouses and is the home of the Exeter Maritime Museum (see chapters 7 and 10). Part of the upper canal section is a country park.

Finch Foundry Trust, Sticklepath, Okehampton EX20 2NW. Telephone: 0837 840286.

Former corn and cloth mills became an edge-tool factory in 1814 and it was worked by Finch Brothers until 1960, manufacturing agricultural tools such as billhooks, scythes and shovels. Three waterwheels drove a pair of tilt-hammers, drop-forging hammers, metal-cutting shears, a fan for the forges, a grindstone for sharpening tools and a polishing wheel. The foundry was restored in working order soon after its closure, and there is also a museum (see chapter 7).

Grand Western Canal, Tiverton.

A country park (see chapter 9) follows part of this canal from the basin at Tiverton almost to the Somerset border near Holcombe Rogus. It was built in 1810-14 to join the Bridgwater Canal at Taunton, and the original intention was to create a canal from the Bristol Channel to the English Channel. The Tiverton basin is of interest and is the start for horse-drawn boat trips.

Haytor Granite Quarries and Tramway, near Bovey Tracey.

Haytor is a popular Dartmoor viewpoint (see chapter 2), but there are interesting quarries and tramways on the north side opened in 1820 by George Templer for the London Bridge contract. Within forty years the quarries were disused because of competition from quarries at Swell Tor and Foggintor on western Dartmoor. One last working was for the Devon War Memorial, which stands outside Exeter Cathedral. The Haytor Granite Tramway carried granite 7 miles (11.2 km) down to the Stover Canal (built in 1792 by James Templer to carry ball clay), where it was taken on barges to Teignmouth and thence by ship to London. The tramway had granite plateway rails in sections about 4 feet (1.2 metres) long, and much can be traced across the moor, with points and branches to other quarries at Holwell Tor and beyond. Wagons descended by gravity and were drawn back up by horses. The Templer Way was opened in 1987 and follows the 17 mile (27 km) route from moor to sea.

Heathcoat's textile mill, West Exe, Tiverton.

John Heathcoat, inventor of a bobbinet lace machine, began making lace at Tiverton in 1816. Today his firm manufactures nets, fabrics and industrial fabrics, including parachutes. The original factory burnt down in 1936 but two gate lodges survive. Heathcoat's factory school was built in 1841 in the style of a fifteenth-century house and is now the factory shop. There are also good examples of nineteenth-century workers' terraced houses near the mill.

Hele Mill, Hele Bay, Ilfracombe. Telephone: 0271 63162.

This working watermill is set back from the Watermouth road east of Ilfracombe. It dates from the sixteenth century and is powered by an 18 foot (5.5 metre) waterwheel. There are displays explaining watermills, and wholemeal flour is milled and sold here.

Hexworthy Mine, near Dartmeet, Dartmoor.

Reached by a track, one mile (1.6 km) south of Hexworthy and Huccaby Bridge, the site includes two earlier mines reopened in 1889-97 and 1905-12 for tin. There are traces of dressing floors and a leat and aqueduct to a large stone wheelpit at the Henroost site (SX 660711). This was connected by tramway to more extensive dressing floors at Hooten Wheals (SX 655708).

Lynton and Barnstaple Railway, Lynton to Barnstaple.

A much loved railway of 1 foot 11½ inch (60 cm) gauge worked between 1898 and 1935 serving the then remote Lynton, but trade was lost to motor transport. Its building was inspired by the publisher Sir George Newnes. Much of the winding course can be traced, rising to 1000 feet (305 metres) at Martinhoe Cross (Woody Bay station). Features include the Chelfham viaduct across the Yeo not far from Barnstaple. There are a small museum at the old Barnstaple terminus (see chapter 7) and a model railway on part of the trackbed at Parracombe (see chapter 9).

Haytor Granite Tramway.

Lynton Cliff Railway, Lynton to Lynmouth.

Built in 1890 to connect Lynton with Lynmouth 500 feet (152 metres) below, this useful and interesting funicular railway operates with a water balance, whereby a filled tank in the descending car draws up the other.

Meldon Viaduct, Meldon, near Okehampton.

This wrought iron lattice-girder and pier viaduct was built in 1874 to carry the old London and South Western Railway as it passed around the northern edge of Dartmoor on its way to Plymouth. It is 120 feet (36.6 metres) tall and spans the West Okement valley at SX 565923, just below the Meldon Reservoir and Meldon quarry. Trains for the latter still use the viaduct as a siding.

Merrivale blowing houses, Merrivale, Dartmoor.

There are three ruined blowing houses beside the Walkham river above Merrivale Bridge at SX 553754, 553762 and 552766. Difficult to date precisely, these small structures were for smelting tin won from streamworks on Dartmoor, with water-powered bellows working the furnace. There may be signs of the wheelpit and granite tin moulds. Other examples can be found in many Dartmoor valleys.

Lynton Cliff Railway has been working since 1890.

Morwellham Quay, Tavistock PL19 8JL. Telephone: 0822 832766.

This was once a major port for shipping copper ore on the Tamar, with inclined planes connecting its ore floors to the Tavistock Canal and the mineral railway to the Devon Great Consols mine. Long abandoned, it has been restored to its appearance in the 1860s, with workers in period costume recreating the atmosphere, including an assayer, a blacksmith and a cooper. There are tiled ore floors around the dock, tramways, limekilns, waterwheels, workers' cottages and a museum with exhibits on the port and the Tamar valley. A tramway takes visitors beside the Tamar to the George and Charlotte copper mine, which has underground tableaux explaining the working of the mine. The sailing ketch *Garlandstone*, built in 1909 at James Goss's shipyard on the river bank opposite Calstock, was brought to Morwellham for restoration in 1987. An additional feature of interest is the hydro-electric power station which takes water from the Tavistock Canal.

Newcomen Engine House, Royal Avenue Gardens, Dartmouth.

A preserved atmospheric engine was erected here in Thomas Newcomen's home town in 1963, to mark the three hundredth anniversary of his birth. It dates from the 1720s and is said to be the oldest engine in existence, having first worked at Griff Colliery and last at Hawksbury Junction on the Coventry Canal from 1821 to 1913.

North Street Iron Bridge, Exeter.

The six-arched iron bridge, built in 1834 to carry North Road across a valley in the city of Exeter, is still in use. Castings give the date and makers, Russell and Browns, Blaina Iron Works. Exeter has another iron bridge, a small footbridge at the Close, dated 1814.

Plymouth and Dartmoor Railway, Plymouth to Princetown.

The line was built in 1823 in an attempt to develop the western edge of Dartmoor. Traffic in farm products, peat and granite was envisaged but only the last became important. The line also served the prison at Princetown. It was taken over and relaid to standard gauge as the Princetown Railway (1883 to 1956). Much of its course can be traced, especially to the south of Yelverton where it follows the Devonport and Plymouth leats, and on Dartmoor. Near the Swell Tor quarries (SX 560733) there are sidings and an old bridge over a stream bypassed by the new line. The nearby Fogintor quarry provided granite for Nelson's Column and had a hamlet for its workers and their families.

A tramway and waterwheel at Morwellham Quay.

Rolle or Torrington Canal, near Bideford.

A 6 mile (9.6 km) canal was built by Lord Rolle in 1827 to carry limestone from a sea lock on the river Torridge to a bank of limekilns at Great Torrington. It closed in 1871. The course can be seen from the A350, including an inclined plane near Weare Giffard (SS 476217) and the Beam aqueduct across the Torridge (SS 474209), which is now a drive to Beam House. A large limekiln is at Annery (SS 462228).

Smeaton's Tower, The Hoe, Plymouth.

This was the third Eddystone lighthouse, of 1759, constructed by John Smeaton using dovetailed blocks of granite and Portland stone for the exterior and interior. Its foundation rock became undermined by the sea, and it was replaced by a new lighthouse by Sir James Douglass in 1882. The old tower was dismantled and re-erected on the Hoe, from where its stump and the new lighthouse can be seen on a clear day.

Tamar Valley, near Tavistock.

The Tamar valley was the scene of much mining and related activity in the nineteenth century, on both the Cornish and Devon banks. The tidal river was busy with shipping. North of Morwellham Quay (see above) was the rich Devon Great Consols (SX 426734), worked in 1844-1902 and once the largest copper mine in Europe. Most of its copper ores and arsenic were sent by a private railway for shipment from Morwellham. At one time the mine had 33 waterwheels using water from the Tamar. The stack of the arsenic calciner stands amid an extensive area which remains clear of vegetation north-west of the A390. Downstream from Morwellham was a second arsenic works at Gawton mine (SX 453688), where the flues and leaning stack survive above the river bank. There was a quay here and at Newquay (SX 454695), where there are ruined cottages and limekilns. More limekilns are at Weir Quay (SX 434646), where there are also ruins of the Tamar and Union lead-smelting works. The Calstock viaduct (SX 433686) was built of concrete blocks in 1907 and still carries a branch railway across the Tamar from Bere Alston into Cornwall.

Tavistock Canal, Tavistock to Morwellham.

Along its 4 miles (6.4 km) this small canal has a 1½ mile (2.4 km) tunnel, a short aqueduct, a branch to Mill Hill slate quarries, warehouses at the Tavistock basin and an inclined plane down to the quays at Morwellham. It was built between 1803 and 1817 by John Taylor partly to carry ores from his Wheal Friendship and other mines as well as serving Tavistock. The ambitious tunnel under Morwell Down took many years, although the portals have the date 1803 over them. The

canal carried copper ores, granite, coal and limestone until 1873 but now provides water for a hydro-electric station at Morwellham.

Tumbling Weir, Ottery St Mary.

This is an unusual circular weir at the Ottery Serge Mills of 1790 (now Ottermill Limited). Water not required for the mill's waterwheel cascades into the weir and back to the river. It is signposted off Mill Street, and there is a pleasant walk beside the millstream.

Wheal Betsy, Mary Tavy. National Trust.

A restored pumping-engine house is a conspicuous feature below the A386 road across the edge of Dartmoor just north of Mary Tavy. The mine was worked for lead, silver and zinc in the nineteenth century. Down the valley was Wheal Friendship, a copper mine developed after 1798 by the famous mining engineer John Taylor. It was reworked for arsenic from the late nineteenth century until 1925, and there are extensive ruins of the arsenic plant. Several long leats brought water for power at the surface of the mines.

Left: *Smeaton's Tower on Plymouth Hoe formerly stood on the Eddystone Rock as a lighthouse.*

Below: *The tumbling weir at Ottery St Mary.*

The lonely engine house at Wheal Betsy near Mary Tavy.

9
Other places to visit

The Aquarium, Marine Biological Association, Citadel Hill, Plymouth PL1 2PB. Telephone: 0752 222772.

Overlooking Plymouth Sound from just outside the Royal Citadel, this is one of the best displays of temperate marine fish in Europe. Many of the specimens of fish and other marine life have been caught from the laboratory's own research vessels.

Babbacombe Model Village, Hampton Avenue, Babbacombe, Torquay TQ1 3LA. Telephone: 0803 38669.

Over four hundred models are maintained to a high standard at this popular 4 acre (1.6 ha) site. Themes vary from a busy town centre to a thatched village, with a railway and scenes from rural life, all in a landscaped setting with flowers, shrubs and dwarf conifers. It takes on a new look when the illuminations are lit at dusk.

Bicton Park, East Budleigh, near Budleigh Salterton. Telephone: 0395 68465.

There is much to do and see here. Attractions include the Bicton Woodland Railway, exhibitions, brass-rubbing centre, pets corner, adventure playground and other entertainments. The gardens are described in chapter 6, and the James Countryside Museum in chapter 7.

The Big Sheep, Abbotsham Barton, Abbotsham, Bideford EX39 5AP. Telephone: 02372 72366.

This unusual project, which opened in the spring of 1988, is based on a sheep dairy and wool craft centre. It shows sheep to be the most important domesticated animal in the world. There are walks, picnic areas and a shop selling a wide variety of sheep products.

Bodstone Barton Working Farm and Country Park, Combe Martin EX34 0NT. Telephone: 027188 3654.

Visitors can experience at first hand a wide variety of farm animals, including cows, sheep, goats, pigs, poultry, Shire horses and ponies, as well as daily and seasonal farming activities. There are cart and trailer rides, a nature trail and adventure playground and many other activities.

Buckfast Butterfly Farm, Buckfastleigh TQ11 0DZ. Telephone: 0364 42916.

The Butterfly Farm is next to the car park at the terminus of the Dart Valley Railway. Tropical and exotic plants provide a setting through which the visitor walks observing unusual caterpillars and butterflies. There is a special hatching area, and bees and insects are also seen behind glass.

Buckfastleigh Caves, Russetts Lane, Buckfastleigh.

There are guided walks around these interesting caves, but they are open only at limited times in the summer. There are also a museum, slide show and shop.

Buckfastleigh Steam Railway, The Station, Buckfastleigh TQ11 0DZ. Telephone: 0364 43536.

This is the Dart Valley Railway, run in the spirit of the Great Western Railway. The attractive valley is followed beside the river for 7 miles (11.3 km) via picturesque Staverton to the outskirts of Totnes (there are no connections to British Rail services). At Buckfastleigh, the Steam and Leisure Park incorporates a railway museum, railway yard, workshops, gardens, a picnic area, cinema, miniature railway and children's play area.

Buzzacott Manor, Buzzacott Lane, Combe Martin EX34 0NL. Telephone: 027188 2359.

There are 6 acres (2.4 ha) of landscaped gardens, children's and adventure playgrounds, duck ponds, a gnome garden and garden centre here on the north side of the Combe Martin valley. The manor house is a hotel.

Combe Martin Wildlife Park, Combe Martin. Telephone: 027188 2486.

The wildlife park is in 15 acres (6 ha) of gardens, woodland and lakes, where meerkats, monkeys, otters, raccoons, red deer, seals, wallabies and birds can be seen.

Dartington Cider Press Centre, Shinners Bridge, Dartington, Totnes TQ9 6TQ. Telephone: 0803 864171.

Shops, craft workshops and exhibitions are set in converted stone cider barns. A central feature is a restored cider press. An interesting pair of old limekilns can be seen nearby.

Dartington Crystal, School Lane, Torrington EX38 7AN. Telephone: 0805 22321.

Here is an unusual opportunity to watch the old skill of glass blowing as craftsmen fashion lead crystal tableware. There are an interpretation centre with a working replica of an eighteenth-century glass cone, an exhibition of glassware from 1650 and a video theatre. A shop has a large range of products for sale.

Dartmoor Wildlife Park, Sparkwell, near Plymouth. Telephone: 075537 209.

Over one hundred species of animals and birds can be seen, including lions, tigers, jaguars, wolves, bears, bison, deer and water birds. Visitors may walk among the friendlier animals in a special enclosure. The West Country Falconry Centre is also here, and there are daily shows.

Devon Guild of Craftsmen, Riverside Mill, Bovey Tracey TQ13 9AE. Telephone: 0626 832223.

The Devon Guild of Craftsmen presents changing craft exhibitions and demonstrations in addition to a Museum of Craftsmanship, study centre and shop. The building was not a normal mill, as the waterwheel pumped water to a tank in the tower above.

Devonshire's Centre, Bickleigh Mill, Bickleigh, near Tiverton. Telephone: 08845 419.

The mill is close to Bickleigh Bridge across the Exe at the pretty village of Bickleigh. It was restored in 1972-3 so that the mechanism from the undershot wheel can be seen. Potters, weavers and woodworkers can be seen in the craft workshops. The complex incorporates a nineteenth-century farm where cows are milked by hand and Shire horses provide motive power. A museum has agricultural equipment, an apple crusher and cider press. The Motor Centre contains veteran, vintage and collectors' vehicles of all types. There are also shops, a restaurant, bird gardens and a fish farm.

Donkey Sanctuary, Slade House Farm, Sidmouth EX10 0NU. Telephone: 03955 78222.

Many unwanted and neglected donkeys are rescued and given care and security for the rest of their lives. The charity works to educate the public, and over three thousand donkeys are cared for at its five farms. There is a riding centre for handicapped children.

English Lace School, Oak House, Church Stile, Woodbury, Exeter EX5 1HP. Telephone: 0395 33273.

The lace school organises short lace courses, a four-year diploma in bobbin lace and a biennial competition and exhibition.

Exmoor Bird Gardens, South Stowford, Bratton Fleming, near Barnstaple EX31 4SG. Telephone: 05983 352.

Formal gardens provide a setting in which there are aviaries for exotic birds and lakes for penguins and waterfowl. One enclosure is the home of rheas. There are picnic areas and a playground for children.

Exmoor Brass Rubbing and Hobbycraft Centre, Watersmeet Road, Lynmouth EX35 6EP. Telephone: 0598 52529.

The centre is in a modern building beside the A39, close to the meeting of the West and East Lyn rivers. Visitors have the choice of over a hundred monumental brasses to rub. There is a hobbycraft section and shop.

The steam railway at Buckfastleigh.

Farway Countryside Park, near Colyton EX13 6JL. Telephone: 040487 224 and 367.

The farm has rare and modern breeds of animals and provides a centre for walks through countryside and woodland, with fine views northwards over the Coly valley. There are facilities for pony trekking, a pets enclosure and nature trails. Away to the west on Farway Down are bronze age round barrows (see chapter 3).

Gnome Reserve and Pixie Kiln, West Putford, near Bradworthy, Holsworthy EX22 7XE. Telephone: 040924 435.

This is a place for children and the young at heart. There are over a thousand gnomes and pixies of all sizes in a woodland setting. There is also the Pixies' wild flower trail. At the Pixie Kiln visitors see pottery pixies being made.

Gorse Blossom Miniature Railway Park, Liverton, Newton Abbot TQ12 6JD. Telephone: 062682 361.

The central feature of the woodland park is the 7¼ inch (18.4 cm) gauge steam railway, with unlimited rides, which passes through attractive woodlands and gardens overlooking the Teign valley, 3 miles (4.8 km) north of Newton Abbot. There are also picnic areas, woodland walks, children's play areas, an assault course, a Swiss model railway and a restaurant.

Grand Western Canal Country Park, The Wharf, Canal Hill, Tiverton.

A beautiful 11¼ mile (18.1 km) stretch of canal from the Wharf at Tiverton has been restored by Devon County Council. From here the Grand Western Horseboat Company (telephone: 0884 253345) operates 2½ hour tranquil horse-drawn barge trips to East Manley, where there is an aqueduct over the former railway to Tiverton. Beyond, the canal meanders so that it is crossed three times by the B3391 between Tiverton and Sampford Peverell (see chapter 8).

Hancock's Devon Cider, Clapworthy Mill, South Molton. Telephone: 07695 2678.

The Hancocks have made cider for five generations. It is a seasonal industry, so a film shows the autumn cider pressing. The cider mill can be toured, viewing the hydraulic presses and old equipment on display. Devon farmhouse cider is on sale and there are also a craft shop and picnic area.

HMS Plymouth, Trinity Pier, Millbay Docks, Plymouth. Telephone: 0752 229269.

The last Type 12 anti-submarine frigate, of 2800 tons, was built at Devonport Dockyard in 1961 and taken over by the Warship Preservation Trust in 1988 for preservation and display in her namesake port. The surrender of South Georgia was signed on board during the Falklands conflict. The ship was later heavily engaged in the war. Four bombs hit the ship, but even after a major fire there was no loss of life.

The Grand Western Canal at Tiverton.

Kents Cavern, Wellswood, Torquay. Telephone: 0803 24059.

The cavern is justly famous for its natural features and important finds dating back 100,000 years showing evidence of early man and extinct animals such as mammoth, sabretoothed tiger, rhinoceros and cave bears. There is a small display of animal bones in the entrance but the main collection is at Torquay Museum (see chapter 7). During a half-mile (0.8 km) tour, lights are used to great effect to illuminate the beautiful coloured stalactites, stalagmites and cascades in chambers such as the Organ Chamber and Stalagmite Grotto.

Kitley Caves, Yealmpton, near Plymouth PL8 2JH. Telephone: 0752 880202.

The caves lie just west of Yealmpton in an attractive setting beside the river Yealm. Bones of prehistoric bears, elephants and hyenas have been found here. A small museum displays these and other finds, including fashioned flints showing that prehistoric man inhabited the caves. The site also has a river walk, woodland trail and picnic area.

Loddiswell Vineyard, Lilwell, Loddiswell, Kingsbridge TQ7 4EF. Telephone: 0548 550221.

There are guided tours and walkabouts of this vineyard, which was first planted in 1977. Visitors also see the winery where the grapes are pressed and wine is produced for bottling. The processes of vineyard management are explained on the tours and by a video film show. Wines can be tasted and purchased in the sampling room and shop.

Lynton and Barnstaple Garden Railway, Fair View, Church Town, Parracombe EX31 4RJ. Telephone: 05983 478.

This working scale-model railway, landscaped to show the old Lynton and Barnstaple Railway at Parracombe, will interest lovers of that line. There is an attractive walk along a short stretch of the original trackbed, across a wooded embankment with wild flowers.

The Milky Way, Downland Farm, Clovelly, Bideford EX39 5RY. Telephone: 02373 255.

There are two major attractions at this Devon farm, just off the A39 to the south-east of Clovelly. Visitors can watch cows being milked from a gallery above the parlour or mix with the baby farm animals and help bottle-feed them or even hand-milk a cow. The Pidler Countryside Collection provides a contrast as it contains old agricultural machinery and implements once used on north Devon farms. Most activities are under cover but there are also a picnic area and adventure playground.

Miniature Pony Centre, Worm Hill Farm, North Bovey, Newton Abbot TQ13 8RG. Telephone: 06473 2400.

Here is the Kerswell Stud of Miniature Shetland ponies, on a farm beside the B3212 road 3 miles (4.8 km) west of Moretonhampstead. Visitors can wander among the ponies and miniature animals such as Dexter cows, pygmy goats, Shetland sheep, miniature donkeys and Vietnamese pot-bellied pigs. Pony rides are available.

National Shire Horse Centre, Dunstone, Yealmpton, Plymouth PL8 2EL. Telephone: 0752 880268.

A feature of the centre is the parade arena where magnificent Shire horses are paraded three times daily in the summer. Adults and foals can be seen in the stables, and alongside are a blacksmith and craft centre. Additional attractions are butterfly and falconry centres, the latter giving flying displays. For the children is Adventure World with a free-fall slide and other features. Special events such as fairs and rallies take place during the year.

North Devon Farm Park and British Sheep Centre, Marsh Farm, Landkey, Barnstaple EX32 0NN. Telephone: 0271 830255.

Unspoilt countryside provides a home for rare breeds of sheep, cattle, goats and poultry. There is also a deer park. The British Sheep Centre has the world's only collection of 49 breeds of British sheep. A countrylife section has rural bygones and a large collection of sheep fleeces. Beyond the fields are woodland walks and disused limekilns, once important for the agricultural communities of north Devon.

Once Upon a Time, Old Railway Station, Woolacombe. Telephone: 0271 870999.

This is a children's theme park, with adventure trails and train rides into a world of fantasy and fairyland. It makes an interesting use of the old Woolacombe station on the Ilfracombe branch railway.

Paignton and Dartmouth Steam Railway, Paignton Station. Telephone: 0803 555872.

Steam trains run from Paignton station in the tradition of the Great Western Railway.

The 7 mile (11.2 km) line passes the superb Torbay coast before crossing inland to follow the wooded Dart estuary to Kingswear, from which a ferry crosses to Dartmouth. The railway survived from 1864 until 1972, when the Dart Valley Light Railway took it over to operate steam trains. The Paignton Model Railway is in the exhibition hall at the steam railway station.

Paignton Zoo, Totnes Road, Paignton TQ4 7EU. Telephone: 0803 557479.

This famous zoo is set in 75 acres (30 ha) of attractive botanical gardens on the outskirts of Paignton. There are some three hundred species of world animals on view including the rare and endangered, and the tropical houses contain exotic plants, birds and reptiles. The unique Ark Family Activity Centre provides an opportunity to learn about animals at first hand. The Jungle Express is a (seasonal) miniature railway around the lake and Gibbon Island.

Parke Rare Breeds Farm, Parke, Bovey Tracey TQ13 9JQ. Telephone: 0626 833909.

Rare breeds of dairy and beef cattle, horses, sheep, pigs and poultry can be seen. Children can experience the tamer animals in the pets corner. The farm is adjacent to the parkland in the Bovey valley with good walks (see chapter 6).

Pecorama Pleasure Gardens and Exhibition, Beer, Seaton EX12 3NA. Telephone: 0297 21542.

The Pecorama Pleasure Gardens are on the western slopes above Beer and provide views over Lyme Bay. A miniature steam and diesel railway passes through the landscaped

The Devonport-built HMS 'Plymouth' is now preserved at Plymouth.

grounds. The gardens also contain a picnic area, a stage for live entertainment in school summer holidays, putting greens, crazy golf and an activity area for children. Indoors a model railway exhibition features many layouts and gauges.

Plymouth Dome, The Hoe, Plymouth PL1 2NZ. Telephone: 0752 603300.
This attraction on the Hoe celebrates the place of Plymouth as a major seaport in world history and wartime. Modern presentation techniques bring to life an Elizabethan street and quayside and some epic sea voyages made from Plymouth. The dockyard, liner traffic, lighthouse, defences and all other aspects of this seaport are included in the displays. An observation gallery with satellite and radar facilities overlooks Plymouth Sound.

Plym Valley Railway, Marsh Mills Station, Coypool Road, Marsh Mills, Plymouth PL7 4NL. Telephone: 0752 330478.
The Marsh Mills to Plymbridge section of the Tavistock Railway is being relaid for the working of restored steam locomotives. The first to be steamed, in 1987, was a saddle tank which spent its working life at Falmouth docks in Cornwall. There are other locomotives and rolling stock, including the largest steam locomotive in Europe, the Beyer Garrat number 4112, which worked on the South African Railways.

Powder Mills Forge, near Two Bridges, Dartmoor.
This remote site is just north of the B3312 between Two Bridges and Postbridge. A terrace of cottages associated with the ruined gunpowder works (see chapter 8) has been restored, and there is now the highest wrought iron smithy in England, at 1200 feet (366 metres).

Quince Honey Farm, North Road, South Molton EX36 3AZ. Telephone: 07695 2401.
The wonderful sight of thousands of bees at work in their hives is presented in a most original manner, all behind the safety of glass. It is an educational experience and the unique opening hives reveal the heart of the colony at work. This is a commercial farm, with a large indoor honeybee apiary. Natural honey and beeswax products are on sale.

Seaton Tramway, Harbour Road, Seaton EX12 2NQ. Telephone: 0297 21702.
A unique narrow-gauge electric tramway with open-topped double-deck tramcars runs beside the saltmarshes of the river Axe, famous for bird life, northwards from Seaton to Colyford and Colyton (see chapter 10).

Shaldon Wildlife Trust, Ness Drive, Shaldon TQ14 0HP. Telephone: 0626 872234.
The trust is a breeding centre for rare small mammals, reptiles and exotic birds. Species here include some of the world's smallest and rarest monkeys.

Silverlands, Stokelake, Chudleigh, Newton Abbot TQ13 0EH. Telephone: 0626 852872.
This all-weather family attraction is set in 15 acres (6.1 ha). Displays and exhibitions include a model circus and craft workshops. There are adventure playgrounds, picnic areas, an animal meadow and tea rooms.

Totnes Heavy Horse Omnibus Centre, Steamer Quay, Totnes. Telephone: 0803 863149.
The centre has Victorian double-decker omnibuses, stables and smithy, and a horse-drawn omnibus service operates to the town.

Watermouth Castle, Berrynarbor, Ilfracombe EX34 9SL. Telephone: 0271 63879.
A castellated castle was built in 1825 as a home for the Basset family, standing in landscaped grounds overlooking Watermouth Harbour. Today both the castle and gardens are a major attraction including a wide variety of imaginative amusements for all the family.

Wheel Craft Workshops, Town Mills, Clifford Street, Chudleigh. Telephone: 0626 852698.
The former mill retains its waterwheel but now houses workshops for craftspeople as diverse as a blacksmith, shoemaker, dressmaker, leatherworker, artist and furniture designer. Craft items are for sale and there is a restaurant.

Wonderful World of Miniature, Sea Front, Exmouth EX8 2AY. Telephone: 0395 278383.
This is the world's largest 00 gauge model railway complex, with up to twenty trains running over 7500 feet (2286 metres) of indoor track, landscaped as countryside, villages and town, and 1500 feet (450 metres) of track outdoors around a 100 foot (30 metre) fish pool.

Yelverton Paperweight Centre, Leg O' Mutton, Yelverton PL20 6AD. Telephone: 0822 854201.
This unusual collection contains over eight hundred antique and modern glass paperweights of all shapes, sizes and colours. A wide selection is for sale.

10
Towns and villages

APPLEDORE
Early closing Wednesday.

This delightful place looks out over the Taw-Torridge estuary and the harbour bar. A quayside road gives access to the water, and narrow streets lead up into the village, where the North Devon Maritime Museum can be found in Odun Road (see chapter 7). In the days of sail Appledore was a busy maritime centre with shipbuilding and many locally owned vessels, but now the quay is quieter. The historic Richmond dry dock of the 1850s has closed, but there is an active shipbuilding yard upstream with an expertise in dredgers and other specialist ships. Across the water is **Instow**, a popular village with a quay and beach.

ASHBURTON
Early closing Wednesday.

This once prosperous stannary and wool town is a good centre for exploring southern Dartmoor. East, West and North Streets meet at the bottom of the town, where the small museum can be found (see chapter 7). Here also is an old arch remaining from the Mermaid Inn, where Fairfax lodged in January 1646 after driving the Royalists from the town. Further up North Street is the austere Town Hall with a bell tower. In West Street the fifteenth-century church (St Andrew) was heavily restored by G. E. Street in the 1880s, but the old tower remains impressive. Opposite the handsome Golden Lion Hotel, at the corner of East Street and Roborough Street, is a conduit of grey limestone.

AXMINSTER
Early closing Wednesday; market day Thursday.

This market town in the Axe valley is well known for its carpets, first manufactured here in 1755. The present factory in Woodmead Road is open to visitors. The town encircles the church (St Mary) with a central tower, on the site of a Saxon minster founded in AD 786. The museum is in Church Street (see chapter 7), and next door is an archway said to be from Newenham Abbey, which lay south of the town. Axminster has several Georgian and Victorian buildings, among them Oak House in Chard Street built in 1758 by Simon Bunter, a lawyer. Thomas Wakley, who founded the medical journal *The Lancet* in 1823, was born at **Membury**, 3 miles (4.8 km) north.

BAMPTON
Early closing Thursday.

A tree-clad castle motte overlooks this small town from the north. Brook Street is wide and the most interesting. The church (St Michael and All Angels) has a rood screen and window glass of about 1495, restored as a war memorial. A stone on the west side of the tower copies a memorial to a clerk's son who was killed by an icicle in 1776. The Exe valley is reminiscent of the Wye, but Bampton is in the valley of the tributary Batherm, where quarrying has been important for many years.

BARNSTAPLE
Early closing Wednesday; market days Tuesday and Friday.

Barnstaple is the major centre for north Devon, a market town and former port on the tidal Taw. Of its Norman castle only the motte survives (see chapter 4), but the street pattern retains the outline of the old town. The castle mound overlooks the new library and information centre and the cattle market. From here it is a short distance past the former Town

Queen Anne's Walk, Barnstaple.

71

The Pannier Market, Barnstaple.

Station, with its small museum in a signal box (see chapter 7), to a pleasant riverside walk along the Great Quay. Here Queen Anne's Walk is a seventeenth-century colonnaded arcade, with the Tome Stone, where merchants settled bargains. The sixteen-arched Long Bridge across the Taw was first built in the thirteenth century but has been rebuilt several times. On the south side are the terminus of the railway from Exeter and the large North Devon Leisure Centre. At the north end of the bridge is The Square, off which Litchdon Street has the seventeenth-century Penrose Almshouses.

The High Street passes through the centre of the old town, where the Guildhall of 1826 stands in front of the large Pannier Market, well worth visiting on market days. Alongside is Butchers Row. Hidden away is St Peter's church with its twisted spire. Behind this trees shade a peaceful haven with the Horwood Almshouses, St Anne's Chapel and the Old Grammar School Museum. Barnstaple has another museum: the Museum of North Devon in The Square (see chapter 7). There are also commercial premises open to visitors, such as Brannam's Pottery in Litchdon Street, established 1879, and Sanders Sheepskin Works and Tannery, Pilton Causeway. Jungleland is a collection of worldwide plants and flowers at St John's Garden Centre, St John's Lane.

Across the Yeo is the attractive village of **Pilton**, a *burh* founded by Alfred in about 880.

At the top of Pilton Street is the interesting Benedictine priory church of St Mary. Its earlier tower was pulled down in the Civil War when it is said the steeple was melted for Royalist cannonballs. There are Victorian almshouses in a Tudor style, but nearby Bull House is authentic.

BEER
Early closing Thursday.

The village of Beer stone and flint houses follows a valley and brook to the shore, where fishing boats are drawn up on a steep pebble beach between the high white chalk cliffs of Beer Head and Seaton Hole. Honiton lace originated here when Flemish refugees arrived in the sixteenth century, and lacemaking has continued ever since. Smuggling was once important too, but Beer is best known for its freestone quarries worked since Roman times. A visit to the underground workings is a memorable experience (see chapter 8). The Pecorama Pleasure Gardens are also here (see chapter 9).

BERE FERRERS
Close to Plymouth, Bere Ferrers is cut off on a triangular peninsula between the Tamar and Tavy estuaries. The shortest route to Plymouth is by the railway, part of the old Waterloo line which crosses the Tavy by a long bridge. By the lanes, the picturesque Denham Bridge crosses the deep Tavy in a wooded valley. The village is in a tranquil setting on

the shore of the tidal Tavy, its church (St Andrew) with effigies of Sir William de Ferrers and his wife Matilda, who restored it in the fourteenth century. The stained glass in the east window is of this period too. **Bere Alston** is at the north of the peninsula, overlooking Calstock on the Cornish side of the meandering Tamar. There were lead-smelting works at Weir Quay, but all is now quiet and the road allows fine views of the estuary.

BIDEFORD

Early closing Wednesday; market days Tuesday and Saturday.

Smaller than Barnstaple, Bideford has a medieval bridge across the Torridge, each of its 24 arches a different size. Traffic congestion on this famous bridge was relieved by the opening of a new high-level bridge downstream in May 1987. At the west end of the bridge is the Town Hall, behind which St Mary's church was rebuilt in 1865 except for the tower. It has a memorial to John Strange, hero and victim of the 1646 plague, when he became mayor for the fourth time after all others had fled. A memorial to Sir Richard Grenville giving his last words was erected in 1891, the tercentenary of his noble death. Bideford has a long maritime tradition, and Grenville came from here. The Quay is still used by coasters loading clay from Petrockstow, and the *Oldenburgh* sails from here to Lundy (see chapter 1). Allhalland and other narrow shopping streets are behind the Quay. The wider Bridgeland Street has bow-windowed houses of 1690, now offices. The Burton Art Gallery (see chapter 7) is in Kingsley Road, at the end of which is a statue

Bideford Bridge over the Torridge.

of Charles Kingsley, who lived here and made the district famous with his writings. The riverside Victoria Park has guns said to have been captured from the Armada in 1688. Across Bideford Bridge is East-the-Water, once an important shipping place. A park on the hill contains a war memorial and Chudleigh Fort (see chapter 4).

BOVEY TRACEY

Early closing Wednesday.

The town is a centre for exploring Dartmoor, with Haytor not far distant to the west. At Parke are the National Park headquarters and interpretative centre, woodland walks and a rare breeds farm (see chapters 6 and 9). To the east of Bovey Bridge the church (St Thomas of Canterbury) has a rood screen and a decorated stone pulpit of the fifteenth century. Beside the bridge, the Devon Guild of Craftsmen has a centre in the Riverside Mill (see chapter 9). Ball clay is extracted to the south and exported from Teignmouth, formerly via the Stover Canal. The clay gave rise to pottery, brick and tile works.

BRADNINCH

The village lies amid hilly farming country on the old road from Exeter to Taunton. In the square the foundation stone of the guildhall was laid in 1921 by Edward, Duke of Cornwall, for the Duchy has estates in the district. The High Street and tree-lined Fore Street descend from here. Off Fore Street the church of St Disen has a crenellated tower with gargoyles, tall Beer stone arcades and a sixteenth-century rood screen. Lower down is Hen Street with a raised pavement, roadside stream and the thatched Comfort House dated

Brixham is an important fishing port.

1681. The Manor House of 1547 is off Parsonage Street but not visible from the road.

BRADWORTHY
This small north Devon village is remarkable for its enormous square, said to be one of the largest in England.

BRAUNTON
Early closing Wednesday.

A large village on the Caen river at the head of Braunton Pill, Braunton lies between Barnstaple and the coast at Braunton Burrows. The parish church of St Brannock is in a large churchyard beside the river at the north end of the village, solid with heavily buttressed tower and spire and a large nave. The Braunton and District Museum is in the old church house (see chapter 7), and there is an art and craft exhibition in the Elliott Gallery at Hills View. To the south-west, Field Lane leads to the Braunton Great Field, a system of open strip fields, said to have survived since medieval times. The Royal Air Force airfield at Chivenor is nearby, with frequent training flights over the Taw estuary.

BRIXHAM
Early closing Wednesday.

An important fishing town, Brixham clings to the sides of two valleys where they meet the sea at the south end of Torbay. Interest is centred on the fishing harbour, tucked in behind Berry Head and protected by the outer breakwater. Brixham is a trawler port and the Brixham Trawler Race in June is a popular annual event. On the Strand the Old Market House has the tourist information office and British Fisheries Museum (see chapter 7). Nearby stands a statue of William of Orange, erected two hundred years after he landed here in 1688. On the New Pier of 1804 are an obelisk and a preserved piece of stone said to be where William first set foot in England. From here visitors can view the New Fish Quay and the outer breakwater, while in Overgang Road the Royal National Mission to Deep Sea Fishermen has an exhibition in the summer. Fore Street leads from the Strand to Bolton Cross, with steep steps rising on the south side. Cavern Steps lead to Bone Cavern, where prehistoric bones and implements have been found. At Bolton Cross are the Town Hall of 1886 and the Brixham Museum (see chapter 7). Market Street and Middle Street lead back to the harbour on the north side of the valley, but it is worth exploring the narrow streets on the slopes above. Here is All Saints' church, where Henry Francis Lyte was vicar and wrote the famous hymn 'Abide with Me', played on the church bells each evening. St Mary's is the medieval church in Upper Brixham. To the south-east, Berry Head is a country park (see chapters 2 and 4).

BROADHEMBURY
This pretty village of thatched cottages lies north-west of the great Hembury hillfort (see

chapter 3). There is a fifteenth-century priest's house near St Andrew's church. Augustus Toplady, who wrote the hymn 'Rock of Ages', was vicar here from 1768 until his death.

BUCKFASTLEIGH
Early closing Wednesday.

This small market town grew as a wool town, although the last woollen mill closed in 1975. In Chapel Street a row of wool workers' cottages has wooden shutters along the top storey. The spired Holy Trinity church is outside the town on a hill reached by a lane or 196 cobbled steps. In the churchyard is the tomb of Sir Richard Cabell, whose vicious black hounds are said to have inspired Conan Doyle's *Hound of the Baskervilles*. The limestone hill has been quarried for stone and has caves where the remains of prehistoric animals have been found. There are caves at the top of Russetts Lane (see chapter 9), and Buckfast Abbey and the Buckfastleigh Steam Railway (see chapters 5 and 9) are nearby.

BUDLEIGH SALTERTON
Early closing Thursday.

This small resort, with genteel villas on the south-facing slopes and west cliff, developed without the benefit of the railway, which came rather later in 1897. Fore Street descends a valley almost parallel to the coast to meet the Marine Parade along a broad bay with a pebbly beach where small fishing boats are drawn up. To the west are high red cliffs, and to the east the mouth of the Otter. The town has a thatched museum and art gallery (see chapter 7).

CHAGFORD
Early closing Wednesday.

Chagford was once a Dartmoor stannary, wool and market town. The much restored market cross in the square has granite piers, and the granite church (St Michael) has an elaborate monument to Sir John Wyddon (died 1575). Chagford became an important centre for exploring the moor in Victorian times, when several new houses were built. There were horse-bus services to the nearest railways at Moretonhampstead and Yeoford, and local moorland guides included James Perrott, who placed the first of the 'letter boxes' (a bottle) at remote Cranmere Pool. Kestor and its surrounding prehistoric monuments lie to the west (see chapter 3).

CHUDLEIGH

This ancient wool town received a charter in 1309. Much was rebuilt after a fire in 1807. The long Fore Street once carried the A38 but this now bypasses the town. The church (St Martin and St Mary) contains a screen with painted panels and a monument to Sir Pierce Courtenay, the great grandfather of Thomas Clifford, who became Lord High Treasurer and built Ugbrooke Park (see chapter 6). The Wheel Craft Workshops are at an old mill in the town (see chapter 9). The limestone Chudleigh Rocks rise from trees to the south and are popular with rock climbers.

The thatched buildings of Lloyds Bank in Chagford.

CHULMLEIGH

The village on the old high road between Crediton and Barnstaple was a borough belonging to the Courtenays until 1539 but declined when the new road was built through the Taw valley. It has all the appearance of a small town which never quite succeeded. The church (St Mary Magdalene) has a tall pinnacled tower, a long rood screen restored in 1914 and good wagon roofs with angels at the bases of the ribs. Sir Thomas Fairfax worshipped here in February 1645 and a helmet on the north wall is of this period. At the end of Fore Street an iron pump with a lamp on top was made in Barnstaple.

CLOVELLY

A world-famous village, Clovelly is glorious in springtime but extremely busy in the summer. A long cobbled street descends between pretty cottages far too steeply for vehicles, so donkeys are used. At the bottom the arm of the harbour wall protects a small anchorage and rocky beach, where there is an old limekiln. Clovelly Court is the seat of the owners of this unique village. Back at the top of the cliffs is the superb Hobby Drive through the woods from the A39, while the iron age

The cobbled street in Clovelly.

Clovelly Dykes (see chapter 3) attests the long history of the area. Just east is the tinier and less visited **Buck's Mills**, with limekilns on the beach, one like a small fort.

COCKINGTON

This tiny village of thatch is almost too pretty to be true. It was bought in 1935 by Torquay Corporation and, being so close to that resort, is busy with visitors. Horse-drawn carriages complete the scene. The village has a mill pond, forge, weaver's cottage and the thatched Drum Inn, designed by Edwin Lutyens in 1934. The attractive Cockington Court dates back to Elizabethan times, and next to it the fifteenth-century church (St George and St Mary) has misericords saved from St Saviour's church in Torquay.

COLYTON

This village of Saxon origins lies on a slope above the Coly, a branch of the Axe valley, and has narrow winding streets and interesting stone houses. Among them are the vicarage of 1529, now named Brereward House after its builder, Old Church House (1612) in the Market Place, and Great House in South Street, home of the Yonge family. The large thatched Colyton Cottage at the end of Queen Street is dated 1610. St Andrew's church is noted for its octagonal lantern tower. Monuments include a restored Saxon cross of about AD 900, the tomb of Margaret Beaufort, Countess of Devon and granddaughter of John of Gaunt (died 1449), and others in the Yonge and Pole chapels, notably that of Sir John and Lady Elizabeth Pole (died 1658 and 1628). Off King Street is an oak-bark tannery with a shop open to the public. The Seaton Tramway (see chapter 9) terminates off Cowhayne Lane, just to the south-east.

COMBE MARTIN

Early closing Wednesday.

The village is spread out along a main street for 1½ miles (2.4 km) down a valley with field strips on either side, best appreciated from a distance. At the bottom is a partly sheltered cove where sailing vessels once landed cargoes on the beach. The coast around Combe Martin Bay is dramatic (see chapter 2). The church (St Peter ad Vincula) has a substantial buttressed tower with figures in niches and a carved and painted rood screen. The most unusual building is the Pack of Cards Inn, with 52 windows and thirteen doors on four floors. The Motor Cycle Collection (see chapter 7) is in Cross Street. The district was important for lead and silver mining as far back as Edward I's time, and Royalist silver coins were minted here in the Civil War. The ruined nineteenth-century Knap Down Mine is above the village on the north side.

CREDITON
Early closing Wednesday.

An old market town, once important for clothmaking, Crediton was too close to Exeter to have developed further. The long main thoroughfare descends through the town. The High Street has nothing earlier than the red-brick Georgian and Victorian buildings, erected following two disastrous fires in the eighteenth century. The fine church (see chapter 5) at the lower end of Crediton proclaims the religious importance of the town, for there was a bishopric here for over a century until 1050, when Exeter took over. Much earlier St Boniface (or Winfrid) was born here in 680 and became a missionary in Germany, where he was martyred. At the top of the town, St Lawrence Chapel of about 1200 was much restored in 1920 and is now a school chapel.

CULLOMPTON
Early closing Thursday.

Cullompton is the principal town in the Culm valley, the M5 now takes the heavy traffic away from its once congested main thoroughfare. As a market town it grew prosperous on the wool trade, which is evidenced by the richly decorated church, one of Devon's finest (see chapter 5). The wide tree-lined High Street curves into the narrower Fore Street, which has two notable buildings. The timbered Manor House Hotel was begun in 1603, and next door Walronds is of a similar date but of sandstone with two wings. These survived a fire of 1839 which destroyed much of the old town centre.

DARTMOUTH
Early closing Wednesday and Saturday; market days Tuesday and Friday.

An ancient town on the west side of the deep-water harbour of the Dart estuary, Dartmouth was once important for exporting cloth and importing wine and later for the fish trade with Newfoundland. The most interesting buildings are around the Quay, an inner basin, and many are former merchants' houses. The Royal Castle Hotel was a coaching inn from Drake's time. The Butterwalk in Duke Street dates from 1635-40, with carved timbers leaning back on granite pillars. Bombed in the Second World War, it was restored and reopened in 1953 and the first floor contains the Dartmouth Museum (see chapter 7). The Market Square is dominated by the Methodist church, rebuilt in 1938. Within the square the Old Market was erected in 1838-9 on land reclaimed from an old mill pool. It is enclosed with side colonnades, and a cobbled floor surrounds the Old Market House in the centre. The Henley Museum (see chapter 7) is in Anzac Street, at the end of which is the superb St Saviour's church (see

Colyton church has an unusual lantern tower.

chapter 5). The town's famous engineer, Thomas Newcomen, is remembered by Newcomen Road and one of his engines preserved at the Royal Avenue Gardens (see chapter 8).

Bayard's Cove gives a view out of the harbour mouth, and on the quay are the Customs House and a neat terrace of houses. A plaque commemorates the sailing of the *Mayflower* and *Speedwell* after anchoring here for repairs in 1620. Nearby are a harbour fort (see chapter 4) and the timbered Agincourt House dated 1380. Returning along the waterfront, the new South Embankment is ideal for watching the harbour, alive with boats and in the summer the regatta. Beyond, the North Embankment has a small memorial recording the sailing of 485 amphibious ships of the United States Navy on 3rd June 1944, the last of many expeditions to sail from the port since the Crusades. At the end cars may cross by the Higher Ferry, a paddler guided by wires. From here the scene is dominated by the imposing Britannia Royal Naval College (1899-1905). Pleasure boats offer harbour cruises and a beautiful river trip up the Dart to Totnes.

Kingswear clings to a steep slope across the

The cobbled quay at Bayard's Cove, Dartmouth.

harbour from Dartmouth and has a marina. It had Dartmouth's closest rail link, which is now a preserved steam railway to Paignton (see chapter 9). Near the Quay at Dartmouth the old Great Western Railway terminus for the passenger ferry from the station is now a restaurant. The quaint Lower Ferry transports cars across the harbour to and from Kingswear.

DAWLISH
Early closing Thursday and Saturday.

Dawlish is well known for the Exeter to Plymouth railway (Brunel's South Devon Railway) which traverses the Devon coast behind the sea-wall promenade and disappears and reappears along the red sandstone cliffs. There is a small pier with a view towards Teignmouth and the conspicuous Parson and Clerk Rock. The stream of Dawlish Water enters the sea under a low railway bridge close to the station. The stream has weirs and ponds, with black swans, and the Lawn park separates the Strand from Brunswick Place, both with architecture from Regency times, when Dawlish developed as a minor resort. Brunswick Place is on the south side and has a 30 foot (9.1 metre) diameter iron waterwheel at the site of the former Strand or Torbay Mills. Barton Terrace has genteel villas, now guesthouses and hotels. The museum is here, at Knowle House (see chapter 7). The church (St Gregory) in Church Street has been restored. The churchyard has an extraordinary family tomb enclosed with a pillared and arched wall of coloured stones, erected in the

century for the Hoares of nearby Luscombe Castle, a large house built by John Nash in about 1800 for the banker Charles Hoare. Church Street leads into Old Town Street on the north side of the valley, off which is The Manor, now council offices. Manor Gardens, a second park, incorporates a leat to the old mills. The High Street runs uphill and parallel to the Strand. Most unexpected at the east end is a thatched house of 1539.

DITTISHAM

Dittisham is a village of pretty cottages alongside a steep lane descending to the Dart estuary, where a passenger ferry crosses to Greenway Quay on the east bank. The river here provides a popular anchorage for yachtsmen. The church (St Peter) is situated above the main village, at a high position inside a meander which gives glimpses down to the river on both sides. It has a fine rood screen and a carved stone pulpit of note.

EXETER
Market days Monday and Friday.

The administrative centre for Devon, Exeter is a city full of architectural interest, despite the destruction of much of the old heart during the air raids of 1942. The Roman town wall (see chapter 3) was repaired and strengthened in medieval times, and much survives, but not the four gateways. The centrepiece is the Cathedral (see chapter 5), part surrounded by attractive buildings in the Cathedral Yard and Close. In the latter a jeweller's shop now occupies Mol's Coffee

House (1596). Next door is St Martin's church, founded in 1065 and one of the many small churches still within the old city. St Stephen Bow and St Petrock are others in the nearby High Street. At the end of the Close and outside the city wall are fine Georgian and Victorian terraces along the broad Southernhay. Returning past the top of Princesshay and High Street, there are guided tours to the Underground Passages, built for water supply possibly by the Romans but enlarged in the middle ages. At the north corner of the city wall, the Crown Courts are on the site of Rougemont Castle but its early Norman gatehouse survives (see chapter 4). Rougemont House is a costume museum (see chapter 7) and has attractive gardens formed from the moat. Outside the city wall are Northernhay Gardens, first laid out in 1612 as one of the earliest public gardens in England. It is a short descent to Queen Street, which has the Royal Albert Memorial Museum (see chapter 7) and the classical front of the Higher Market (1838), which hides a modern shopping development.

Back in the High Street, the Guildhall is one of the oldest municipal buildings still in use. It

Right: *Mol's Coffee House in the Cathedral Close at Exeter.*

Below: *The Custom House on the Quay at Exeter.*

is open to the public and the city's silver and regalia are on display. The front of 1592 is supported on granite pillars over the pavement, and behind is a fifteenth-century hall. After crossing North and South Streets, the main thoroughfare descends into Fore Street. On the north side is St Olave's church, rebuilt in the fifteenth century with a tiny tower and restored in 1815. It had links with St Nicholas Priory (see chapter 6), reached along The Mint, a narrow passage where coins were minted in 1696. Tuckers Hall is next, belonging to the Guild of Weavers, Fullers and Shearmen, for Exeter was once an important centre for the wool and cloth trade. Behind the restored front of 1905 is a hall with an arched braced roof of 1471 and oak panelling of 1634. Nearby, the cobbled Stepcote Hill is attractive with period buildings, and St Mary Steps church has a clock with figures called Matthew the Miller and his sons.

It is a short descent to the Quay with its Custom House of 1681, nineteenth-century warehouses and fishmarket. The Quay House Interpretation Centre is in a restored seventeenth-century building and explains the growth of the city and port of Exeter. The historic Butts Ferry is pulled across on a wire

The Guildhall, Exeter.

to the Exeter Maritime Museum at the Canal Basin (see chapter 7). The whole area is fascinating and a footpath follows the canal to the Exe estuary.

To the north of the city centre are the University and Northcott Theatre, set in pleasant surroundings. In the other direction the Devonshire Regiment Museum (see chapter 7) is off Topsham Road. Beyond the city at Clyst Honiton is Exeter's regional airport, and the Devon County Show is held at Clyst St Mary every May.

EXMOUTH
Early closing Wednesday.

Exmouth is a busy resort and port at the mouth of the Exe estuary. The lengthy Esplanade overlooks a sandy beach as far as low red cliffs at the east end. Behind are the low dunes of The Maer. The Plantation and Madeira Walk form a pleasant park beneath trees and above is The Beacon, a row of Georgian houses where Lady Byron and Lady Nelson once stayed. Off Rolle Road the church (Holy Trinity) is impressively tall and its tower dominates Exmouth. The interior is almost of cathedral proportions, and carved wood panelling along the nave walls forms a memorial to Exmouth's dead in the First World War. Outside, Bicton Place has an attractive terrace of cottages. The town centre is bustling with shoppers, augmented by holidaymakers in the summer months. Here is the Exmouth Museum, tucked away off Exeter Road (see chapter 7). At the west end of the Esplanade, Exmouth Docks are a focus of interest, busy with coasters. From here one looks across to Dawlish Warren, to which a small passenger ferry runs. This is the narrowest point at the mouth of the Exe and great sand bars are exposed at low tide.

GREAT TORRINGTON
Early closing Wednesday; market days Thursday and Saturday.

This hilltop market town has commanding views. The Town Hall was rebuilt in 1860 and juts out into the short High Street. It contains a small museum (see chapter 7). Set back at the top of the street is the spacious church (St Michael and All Angels) with a spire. It was blown up with powder on 16th February 1645 but rebuilt six years later. Not far away in New Street is Palmer House, where Sir Joshua Reynolds and Dr Samuel Johnson stayed in 1752. At the bottom of the High Street and Square is the Pannier Market of 1842, with the old assembly rooms above, now a library. To the south was a short-lived castle, demolished in 1228 and its site now a bowling green. Castle Hill is a memorable viewpoint, with walks along the top of Torrington Common, which drops steeply to the Torridge. Far below at a

The rugged coast at Hartland.

bridge is Taddiport, where the tiny chapel of St Mary Magdalene was for a leper hospital. In contrast there is a large modern creamery here. Another important industry is the Dartington Crystal factory off School Lane on the north side of town, where guided tours are given (see chapter 9). An annual event is the May Fair, and on the first Thursday of May the May Queen is crowned and there is maypole dancing in the High Street.

HARTLAND

In this large windswept parish at the north-west corner of Devon deep sheltered combes lead down to a rugged coast. Hartland village has narrow streets and a small square. The early Victorian chapel of St John is on the site of a town hall, of which are retained the bellcote and clock dated 1622. Activities here are as diverse as potteries and the British Geological Survey's magnetic observatory. Roads pass this way to Hartland Point and its lighthouse, or to the secluded Hartland Abbey (see chapters 2 and 6) and the lovely parish church at Stoke, 1½ miles (2.4 km) west, before reaching Hartland Quay, where there is a hotel and museum (see chapter 7). The old quay was destroyed by the sea in 1896, so there is only a tiny pier and slip for small boats. The cliffs are dramatic, with steeply inclined strata folded and contorted. Lundy stands up 13 miles (21 km) offshore.

HATHERLEIGH

Early closing Wednesday; market day Tuesday.

This hillside village has a cattle market. The manor was given by Ordgar, Earl of Devon, for the building of Tavistock Abbey, a gift confirmed by Ethelred in AD 981. The steep South Street has some pretty thatched cottages. The church (St John) has a spire and a large interior with sloping floor. It contains an elaborately carved box pew, Flemish glass of 1653 and a memorial to Cradock Glascott, vicar in 1781-1831 and friend of Wesley and Whitefield, the founders of Methodism. Burning tar barrels are carried on a sledge through the streets on 5th November, but this is a tradition older than the Gunpowder Plot.

Hatherleigh Moor to the east has excellent views across to Dartmoor. Near Deckport Cross a granite obelisk and bronze plaque are in memory of Lieutenant Colonel William Morris, a captain at Balaclava, and Lieutenant John Henry Thomson, who fell at that battle in October 1854. Hatherleigh is the main centre in this part of north Devon, and there are several attractive villages around. These include **Winkleigh**, where thatched cottages cluster around the church and there are two castle mounds, and **Northlew**, with a large square and pretty church.

HOLSWORTHY

Early closing Tuesday; market days Wednesday and Thursday.

A market centre for north-west Devon and parts of adjoining Cornwall, Holsworthy is described as a port town, for a branch of the Bude Canal was opened in 1823 to nearby Blagdonmoor Wharf and Holsworthy had its own wharf at Stanbury Cross, where the canal crossed the Bideford road. The church (St Peter and St Paul) has a pinnacled granite tower, a landmark. The central and largest of three squares has a pannier market on

81

Wednesdays. The town has a small museum in the local council offices (see chapter 7).

HONITON
Early closing Thursday; market days Tuesday and Saturday.

An old coaching town with a long broad High Street following the line of the Roman road to Exeter, Honiton is now bypassed by the A30. Most houses were rebuilt after a fire of 1765, but Marwood House at the east end opposite King's Road dates from 1619. This was built by John, son of Thomas Marwood who was physician to Elizabeth I. The Honiton Pottery is at this end of the High Street and can be visited. Further along, the former Allhallows Chapel and grammar school are now the museum (see chapter 7). The neighbouring St Paul's church was built in 1837-8 by Charles Fowler. The old parish church (St Michael) is up a long hill to the south past the railway station. It was rebuilt after a fire of 1911. Copper Castle, a castellated toll house with gates, is on King's Road as the A35 ascends towards Axminster. At the top of the hill is the Bishop's Tower, a folly built in 1842 by Bishop Edward Copplestone, whose country seat was Offwell House.

ILFRACOMBE
Early closing Thursday; market day Saturday.

Apart from the Taw-Torridge estuary this is the only good harbour on the north Devon coast, partly sheltered by a rugged cliff and improved by a quay and outer pier. The fourteenth-century chapel of St Nicholas on the harbour headland, Lantern Hill, has been a lighthouse since 1522. In the nineteenth century there was a brisk coastal trade to the South-west and South Wales. This was largely lost when the railway came in 1874 but was replaced by tourism. In the twentieth century Ilfracombe was a port of call for Bristol Channel pleasure steamers. Old Ilfracombe is behind the harbour but was most developed in the late nineteenth century to become a hilly town of villas, hotels and guest houses on both sides of a steep valley. There are small beaches below the cliffs, but the most interesting is Tunnels Beach, reached by tunnels cut through the solid rock. The museum is at the lower end of town off Wilder Road (see chapter 7). To the east are the historic Chambercombe Manor and Hele Mill (see chapters 6 and 8). A large windmill for generating electricity is a curious landmark on a hill to the west.

IVYBRIDGE
Early closing Wednesday.

Ivybridge has expanded as a dormitory to Plymouth. It is on the Erme as it emerges from Dartmoor, and thus the moor and little hamlet of Harford are easily accessible. The Stowford paper mill was established using water power in 1785 and still produces quality and security papers. The railway viaduct across the valley is another notable monument. The South Dartmoor Leisure Centre is Ivybridge's newest attraction and includes a sports arena and indoor and outdoor swimming pools.

KINGSBRIDGE
Early closing Thursday; market day Wednesday.

At the head of the estuary 4 miles (6.4 km) upstream from Salcombe, Kingsbridge is served by a ferry during the summer. It was once an important port serving a largely agricultural community, but now only the old quays are evidence of this former prosperity. The main Fore Street leads up into the town. At the top of the hill is the Town Hall with a curious onion-domed clock-tower dated 1875. Here is also the Shambles, an eighteenth-century market house raised on granite pillars taken from an earlier building. Behind is the church (St Edmund), cruciform with a central tower and spire. It contains an unusual lectern supported by a rough granite plinth. Notable monuments include one to Frances, wife of John Hawkins of the East India Company, who died in 1817 on passage home from Bombay. Another is to William Duncumbe, first schoolmaster of the Free School, who taught for 28 years until his death in 1698. This Old Grammar School is further up High Street and was endowed in 1670 by Thomas Crispin, a fuller born in Kingsbridge. It is now the interesting Cookworthy Museum (see chapter 7), named after another of the town's sons, William Cookworthy, who first discovered china clay in Cornwall. The ancient ceremony of glove hanging and reading out the fifteenth-century charter takes place at the annual fair in July.

LUSTLEIGH
This village with some thatch is attractively situated on a hillside among trees. The church (St John) has effigies of a thirteenth-century knight and his lady, probably of the Dynham family, but its most interesting relic is a stone of the fifth or sixth century inscribed to Datuidoc son of Conhinoc. A good walk from the village is to Lustleigh Cleave, where boulder-strewn slopes fall 500 feet (152 metres) to the Bovey river.

LYDFORD
Lydford was a defended Saxon *burh* on a promontory between two valleys. Ethelred had a mint here and coins were taken in AD 997 when the Danes sacked the town and burnt the church. It is now a small quiet village, yet it has by far the largest parish on

Dartmoor. It is best known for its gorge and castle (see chapters 2 and 4). Between the two is St Petrock's church on the site of an earlier one. Small windows give a dark interior, where there is a plain tub font of Hurdwick stone and Saxon or early Norman date. Outside near the south porch is the watchmaker's tomb, a slate slab with a poem to George Routleigh, who died 'wound up' in 1802.

LYMPSTONE

Lympstone is well known for the Royal Marines training camp just outside the village, but the old part has intricate narrow streets, little courts and cottages looking across the Exe estuary to Powderham Castle. There is a slipway and tiny harbour against low red sandstone cliffs. A brick Italianate clock-tower was erected on the beach by W. H. Peters in 1885 to commemorate his wife, Mary Jane, and her kindness and sympathy for the poor of the village. The nearby Limekiln House is a reminder of the once important kiln on the beach.

LYNTON and LYNMOUTH
Early closing Thursday.

This part of north Devon was remote before transport facilities improved and has been called the 'English Switzerland'. There is dramatic scenery all about and Lynton is the main centre for exploring the steep wooded valleys on the coastal edge of Exmoor. The Valley of Rocks is a short walk west (see chapter 2). Although the two are separated vertically by 500 feet (152 metres), Lynton and Lynmouth are best grouped together. At the top, Lynton became fashionable in the nineteenth century. The Lyn and Exmoor Museum is in a cottage in the older part of the town (see chapter 7). The ornate Town Hall of 1900 was erected by Sir George Newnes, who also provided the unusual cliff railway to Lynmouth and backed the Lynton and Barnstaple Railway (see chapter 8). Lynmouth suffered a devastating flood in August 1952, when the swollen East and West Lyn rivers swept away houses and 31 people died. The most picturesque part is Mars Hill, a row of thatched cottages. There is a small harbour at the river mouth, and the Rhenish tower on the pier is a curiosity, rebuilt after collapsing in the disaster. The Exmoor Brass Rubbing Centre (see chapter 9) is a little upstream at the meeting of the two Lyn rivers. The Glen Lyn Gorge and Watersmeet are worth visiting on the West and East Lyn rivers (see chapter 2).

MODBURY
Early closing Wednesday.

Modbury is an interesting small town on a hilly site. Church Street climbs steeply with a stepped and raised pavement and attractive houses and shops, some slate-hung. The church (St George) is offset at the top of the town, surrounded by tombstones. It has a mid fourteenth-century tower and spire and damaged effigies of knights and ladies of the Prideaux and Champernowne families, the latter once lords of the manor. At the bottom of Church Street is the rather plain exterior of the eighteenth-century White Hart and Assembly Rooms, and opposite is the sixteenth-century Exeter Inn. Brownston Street climbs east from here past the former Literary and Scientific Institute of 1840, with a classical pillared facade. At the top the long front of the Queen Anne period Traine House has pillars supporting a balustraded balcony, quite unlike anything else in the town. Opposite is a granite conduit of 1708 decorated with pinnacles and balls. Water was also supplied by other less ornate conduits in Church Street and Galpin Street.

MORETONHAMPSTEAD
Early closing Thursday.

This small medieval market town is often described as the gateway to east Dartmoor and in this was greatly assisted by the branch railway from Newton Abbot, which ran from

The Rhenish tower on the pier at Lynmouth.

The almshouses at Moretonhampstead.

1866 until 1964. The church (St Andrew) is on a Saxon site and its tower of 1418 is a local landmark. There are memorials to French officers who died here while on parole during the Napoleonic Wars. The Sentry or Sanctuary Field beyond the church is like a park at the edge of the town. Cross Street, the road to Exeter, has the most interesting building — thatched granite almshouses with columns and a datestone of 1637. The old Mearsden Manor is in the same street, now an art gallery.

NEWTON ABBOT
Early closing Thursday; market days Wednesday and Saturday.

Newton Abbot has been a railway town since the coming of the South Devon Railway from Exeter in 1846. The line continues westward through hilly country via Totnes to Plymouth, while there is a branch to Torquay and Paignton. There are railway and other workers' terraces within the town, and there are villas on the two main wooded hills above. The town centre is some distance from the station. Here a tapering limestone clock-tower is all that remains of the demolished fourteenth-century St Leonard's church. In front is a stone pedestal upon which the first declaration of William III, Prince of Orange, was read by the rector on 5th November 1688. A building nearby is dated 1690, but the town has been much altered. In Bank Street is the impressive building of the Passmore Edwards Public Library, Science, Art and Technical School (1902-3) in pale limestone and ornamental tile. Along Wolborough Street are the Mackrell Almshouses of 1874, a long terrace with yews in front. Beyond, off Totnes Road, is Bradley Manor (see chapter 6). St Mary's church is in Old Totnes Road, but a more interesting church is at Milber to the south-east of the town. Inspired by a dream, this dates from the 1930s and has three converging naves.

Newton Abbot is at the head of the Teign estuary, where the Hackney and Stover canals once brought down clay for export from the Bovey basin. The racecourse is on this low land to the east separating the town from Kingsteignton. Seale Hayne Agricultural College is 2 miles (3.2 km) to the north-west.

NEWTON FERRERS
South-facing, with old fishermen's cottages and more recent development, on a branch of the attractive Yealm estuary, this is a favoured place for yachtsmen and there is a seasonal ferry across the creek to the twin village of Noss Mayo. There are scenic walks on both sides of the estuary (see chapter 2).

OKEHAMPTON
Early closing Wednesday; market day Saturday.

Okehampton is a good centre for exploring the Dartmoor National Park, but until the opening of the A30 bypass in 1988 it was a notorious bottleneck for summer holiday traffic passing to and from Cornwall. The early town was built between the East and West Okement rivers. In Fore Street the fifteenth-century Chapel of Ease is a prominent landmark. The attractive Town Hall was built in 1685 as the town house of local merchant John

Northmore and took on its present role in 1821. The Charter Hall behind was built in 1973 to commemorate the town charter, granted by James I in 1623. Across West Street is the Dartmoor Centre, which includes the Museum of Dartmoor Life (see chapter 7) and tourist information centre. Simmons Park lies on the south side of the town and has attractive walks beneath trees beside the East Okement river. The castle (see chapter 4) is beside the West Okement. The parish church (All Saints) stands on a hill to the north-west and was rebuilt after a fire in 1842. Tors Road climbs steeply on to the wilds of Dartmoor to the south. There is an army camp here, and access to the moor may be restricted when military training is in progress.

OTTERY ST MARY
Early closing Wednesday.

A small town of some charm in the Otter valley, its chief interest is the twin-towered church (see chapter 5). Samuel Taylor Coleridge was born here in 1772 when his father was vicar and master of the grammar school, and there is a small wall plaque outside the church. There are attractive period houses in Silver Street, Cornhill and Paternoster Row as they climb past the church. An old and exciting tradition takes place every 5th November when men carry blazing tar barrels through the streets. To the west of the town centre off Mill Street is the unusual Tumbling Weir (see chapter 8). Cadhay House (see chapter 6) is just outside the town.

PAIGNTON
Early closing Wednesday.

Paignton is known mainly as a popular seaside resort, having developed in the nineteenth century as a neighbour of Torquay, especially after the railway arrived in 1859. The old town of Paignton lies half a mile (0.8 km) inland. The parish church (St John the Baptist) is of red sandstone and stands on the site of a Saxon church and a pagan burial mound. Some Norman work can be seen in the church fabric, including the font. South of the church the Coverdale Tower and some crenellated wall are the remains of the Bishop's Palace founded in the fourteenth century. One incumbent was Miles Coverdale, who translated the Bible into English and who was Bishop of Exeter in 1551-3. There are interesting nineteenth-century buildings in Church Street and a converted brewery in Princes Street. In 1889-97, number 6 Palace Avenue was the home of the pioneering physicist Oliver Heaviside, who worked on radio waves and communications. Kirkham House is a restored medieval town house at the corner of Kirkham Street and Mill Lane (see chapter 6), and the thatched Kirkham and

Chantry Cottages are probably seventeenth-century. Oldway Mansion was begun by Isaac Singer, founder of the sewing-machine company, and some rooms and the formal gardens are open to the public (see chapter 6).

The famous Paignton Zoo (see chapter 9) is on the outskirts of the town towards Totnes. The Paignton and Dartmouth Steam Railway (see chapter 9) starts from Paignton Station and gives superb views of the coast on the way to Kingswear. There are good sandy beaches at Paignton Sands and Goodrington Sands beyond Roundham Head. The former has a pier and promenade backed by the Green and hotels. The small harbour is quite unexpected after the promenade, with fishing and pleasure boats. A regatta is held every August. Further south Elberry Cove is a pebbly beach surrounded by woodland and a complete contrast to the developments at Paignton. Offshore a freshwater spring is sometimes visible.

PLYMOUTH
Early closing Wednesday; market days Monday to Friday.

The original three towns of Plymouth, Stonehouse and Devonport were amalgamated in 1914 to become Devon's largest city lying between the Hamoaze and Cattewater, or lower Tamar and Plym estuaries. A terrible bombing raid in March 1941 destroyed most of the centre of the city, so a brand new one was designed by Sir Patrick Abercrombie with broad streets and avenues. To the north-east the Museum and Art Gallery (see chapter 7) faces the Polytechnic at Drake Circus, while down Charles Street the bombed building and spire of Charles Church (1664) stands in a roundabout as a memorial to Plymouth's war dead. The north-south Armada Way passes through the whole of Abercrombie's development, a belt of green leading up to the famous Hoe. Along the grand Royal Parade is the Civic Centre of 1962, which provides a good viewpoint from the top. The 1874 Guildhall and its neighbour St Andrew's church were bombed and rebuilt after the Second World War and are worth visiting. The former has stained glass illustrating events in Plymouth's history from the fourteenth century to 1953. Behind are two wonderful survivors of old Plymouth, the stone Prysten House (see chapter 6) and the half-timbered Merchant's House, now a museum (see chapter 7).

Below, the Barbican area of old Plymouth has narrow streets full of character, some cobbled. In Southside Street part of a fifteenth-century Dominican friary is now part of Coates and Company's dry gin distillery, which is open for guided tours. In New Street the Elizabethan House has been restored with period furniture (see chapter 6). Around Sutton Harbour are the Custom House, the fish quay and market and a marina. West Pier has the Mayflower Steps and a stone commemorating the departure of the Pilgrim Fathers in 1620. Many other plaques here record famous arrivals and departures over the centuries. The Royal Citadel (see chapter 4) dominates the hill between the Barbican and the Hoe, and just outside its walls is a fine aquarium (see chapter 9).

The Hoe, topped with a wide Promenade, has excellent views of the Sound, a safe anchorage protected by Rennie's great breakwater, and Drake's Island. There is usually some shipping activity to observe and the Sound is the scene of many yachting events. Monuments on the Hoe include the tall naval cenotaph naming hundreds who died in both world wars, and a statue of Sir Francis Drake, for it is here that he is said to have learnt of the Armada while playing bowls. Smeaton's Tower is the old Eddystone lighthouse of 1759 to 1882 and is open to visitors (see chapter 8), as is Plymouth Dome (chapter 9). At the west end of the Hoe Brunel's Millbay Docks are still in use, mainly for ferry services to Brittany and Spain. The preserved frigate HMS *Plymouth* is berthed here (see chapter 9). A towering grain elevator at the West Wharf is a major Plymouth landmark.

To the north is **Stonehouse**, where Union

The statue of Sir Francis Drake on Plymouth Hoe.

Street leads from the Royal Parade and maintains its pre-war plan. From Admiral's Hard a ferry crosses to Cremyll on the Cornish side, where Mount Edgcumbe Park is jointly administered by Plymouth City Council and Cornwall County Council. On Western King Point, at the end of Durnford Street, is Rennie's Royal William Victualling Yard. This is separated by Stonehouse Pool from the huge naval dockyard for which **Devonport** is best known (see chapter 8). A tall granite column commemorates the changing of Devonport's name from Plymouth Dock by royal decree in 1824. Here at the end of Ker Street is also the classical Town Hall, now a library, and Oddfellows Hall in the Egyptian style. All are lucky survivors of the work of the architect John Foulston: many of his streets in Stonehouse and Plymouth were destroyed by bombing. At Mount Wise a park overlooks the Hamoaze and gives close-up views of passing warships. There is a memorial to Robert Falcon Scott of the ill-fated Antarctic expedition in 1910-12.

Plymouth has expanded rapidly and enveloped outer settlements such as **St Budeaux**, where Brunel's famous Royal Albert rail bridge and the modern road bridge cross the Tamar to Cornwall. Central Park is the largest of the city's parks and has many recreational facilities including the indoor Mayflower Centre. Plymouth Airport, north towards Yelverton, has pioneered the use of short-takeoff passenger aircraft for domestic routes. Plympton and Plymstock, across the Laira Bridge, are now part of Plymouth's conurbation.

PLYMPTON

Plympton was once a stannary town, but its two old districts are now enveloped by the eastward expansion of Plymouth. Plympton St Maurice is a pleasant surprise, grouped around the old motte and bailey castle (see chapter 4) and fourteenth-century church. In Fore Street several houses have arcades over the pavement, including the Guildhall of 1688. Near the church, George Lane has the old Grammar School (1664), which the painter Sir Joshua Reynolds (1723-92) attended when his father was master. Sir Charles Lock Eastlake (1793-1865), later President of the Royal Academy and director of the National Gallery, was also a pupil. The large Plympton House of 1700 can be seen further up George Lane. Plympton St Mary is now less distinctive as a settlement. It grew up around the Augustinian priory established in 1121, of which only the church and a Norman doorway remain.

PRINCETOWN

Early closing Monday and Saturday.

Not an attractive place at 1430 feet (436 metres) above sea level and dominated by the prison and housing for its officers, Princetown owes its development to Sir Thomas Tyrwhitt and its name to the Prince of Wales, who owned the land. The austere granite prison was built in 1806-9 for French prisoners of war; later Americans were held here too. Having become disused, it was refurbished in 1850 for British convicts and has remained occupied ever since. St Michael's church was built by French and American prisoners in 1810-15 and has been restored since a fire in 1908. The east window was given by American women in memory of their men who died here. Tyrwhitt's other inspiration to open up Dartmoor was the Plymouth and Dartmoor Railway of 1823 (see chapter 8). Princetown is a centre for walking on this part of Dartmoor and for motorists: Burrator, Dartmeet, Postbridge and Two Bridges are not far.

SALCOMBE
Early closing Thursday.

Salcombe lies near the mouth of the Kingsbridge estuary, in many ways a smaller Dartmouth and popular for yachting and boating. In the 1860s nearly a hundred trading vessels worked from Salcombe, especially in the Azores citrus fruit trade, when the port's schooners became known as 'Salcombe fruiters'. Fishing boats now operate from the Fish Quay near the large Creek car park. The church is Victorian. The very narrow Fore Street follows the shore, with shops and pubs. On Custom House Quay is the museum (see chapter 7), and Normandy Way commemorates the Second World War D-Day preparations and sailings with which the harbour was much concerned. A small ferry crosses to East Portlemouth. Towards the harbour entrance are the ruins of Fort Charles (see chapter 4) and two beaches at North Sands and South Sands, the latter with an old lifeboat station. Beyond are Sharpitor and the Overbecks Museum (see chapters 6 and 7), and a superb clifftop walk to Sharp Tor and Bolt Head at the very mouth of the haven (see chapter 2).

SEATON
Early closing Thursday.

The resort developed on the low land where the Axe valley meets the south-east coast. Its main asset is the fine setting behind a long beach contained between the high chalk cliffs of Seaton Hole in the west and the great landslips of Dowlands in the east (see chapter 2). The Seaton Tramway offers an interesting journey from the town to Colyford and Colyton (see chapter 9). There is a small fishing port at the mouth of the Axe, where a shingle bank almost cuts off the entrance to the estuary. The river is crossed by an early concrete bridge of 1877. **Axmouth** village is of interest on the east bank, with a Norman church and attractive cottages. It was once a thriving port.

SHALDON
Early closing Thursday.

Across the Teign estuary from larger Teignmouth, Shaldon has preserved much of its character. It is a contrast to the bustle of Teignmouth, with homely Regency houses in Fore Street and along Marine Parade. The latter gives excellent views of shipping entering the harbour for Teignmouth docks. At the end the great red sandstone Ness headland is a prominent landmark. Just beyond, the beach at Ness Cove is reached via the Smugglers' Tunnel, a feature dating from Napoleonic times and once used to carry limestone from ships on the beach to the old limekiln at the top. Here also is the Shaldon Wildlife Trust (see chapter 9).

SHEBBEAR

The Devil's Stone under an oak on the green is the point of interest in this north Devon village. This strange boulder is turned over with sticks and levers every 5th November in a curious ceremony accompanied by the ringing of the church bells. Features of the church itself (St Michael) include a Norman doorway, a carved pulpit and an effigy of a fourteenth-century lady.

SIDMOUTH
Early closing Thursday.

The town, where the Sid valley meets the sea, developed as a fashionable resort in Regency times. As a seal of approval, the young Victoria and her parents, the Duke and Duchess of Kent, stayed at the Royal Glen Hotel in 1819. Other famous visitors included Elizabeth Barrett Browning and her family, who stayed at Cedar Shade further back in the town in All Saints Road. Today fishing boats are drawn up on a pebbly beach which is contained between the steep red cliffs of Salcombe Hill to the east and High Peak cliff and rocky stacks to the west. The Esplanade has Regency-style hotels, such as the Royal York with a veranda on pillars. The old part of the town is near the sea with small streets around the Market Place. The church (St Giles and St Nicholas) is of interest and contains a window donated by Queen Victoria in memory of her father. Nearby is the museum (see chapter 7). The attractive Amyatts Terrace looks over tennis courts and the bowling green to Coburg Terrace, which has unusual white crenellated houses. At the end is the Old Chancel, saved by Peter Orlando Hutchinson when the church was restored in 1859, and rebuilt as part of his house. At the top of Salcombe Hill on the east of the town is the Norman Lockyer Observatory. Coastal views extend from Berry Head to Portland, but the best is of the town from Peak Hill. A Folk Festival is held every summer.

SOUTH MOLTON
Early closing Wednesday; market day Thursday.

This market centre lies on the road to Barnstaple, surrounded by farming country. Broad Street is aptly named, and at the west end, or the Square, the Guildhall has an attractive facade of 1743 containing material re-used from the demolished Stowe House near Bude in Cornwall. The old Assembly Room or Dining Room and Mayor's Parlour are notable, while the ground floor contains the museum (see chapter 7). Next door the large Market Hall of 1863 has three carved rams' heads on the front and an assembly room above with an arched roof. The Post Office nearby was built as a corn exchange in 1809. The church (St Mary Magdalene) is approached by narrow cobbled lanes, and its fine buttressed tower dominates the town and is visible for miles. The Congregational church is unusually positioned and faces the tower. The Quince Honey Farm is in North Road (see chapter 9).

SOUTH ZEAL
South Zeal lies up a hill along the old coach road from Exeter to Okehampton. The properties are noted for their long strips of land behind. The all-granite Oxenham Arms has a fine porch and is the best building here, once the home of the Burgoynes in the early sixteenth century. In the middle of the wide street is a simple medieval market cross and St Mary's chapel, rebuilt in 1713 with clock and bell tower. The great bulk of Dartmoor rears up to the south, where there are the old dumps of Ramsley copper mine, last worked in 1901-9. Just west are Sticklepath and the Finch Foundry and museum (see chapters 7 and 8).

STOKE GABRIEL
This pretty village of terraced cottages and villas overlooks a creek of the Dart estuary, artificially ponded by the causeway of a former tide mill. The church (St Mary and St Gabriel) is approached by a cobbled way past the Church House Inn and a nineteenth-century National School house. Inside the church the screen and carved pulpit were restored in 1931. A yew in the churchyard is said to be fifteen hundred years old.

TAVISTOCK
Early closing Wednesday; market days Wednesday and Friday.

Tavistock is a pleasant market, stannary and wool town on the Tavy below the western slopes of Dartmoor, with a popular Goose Fair held every October. There was a Benedictine abbey here from AD 974 until 1539, but only scattered parts remain in Abbey Place and Plymouth Road. The Dukes of Bedford acquired the land and the seventh Duke financed many buildings and workers' houses in the town and neighbourhood, using revenue notably from the rich Devon Great Consols mine in the Tamar valley (see chapter 8). The town centre is Bedford Square, where there is a statue of the Duke in front of the Guildhall of 1848. Next to this is the court gate of the old abbey, and then the fine crenellated Town Hall, which the Duke erected in 1860 using the local green volcanic Hurdwick stone. Behind is a good pannier market, also approached from Duke Street.

Across the square is the large church (St Eustachius), mainly fifteenth-century with lofty granite arcades and a clothworkers' aisle. There is a decorated fragment of the abbey cloister in the churchyard. Betsy Grimbal's Tower is an abbey gateway next to the Bedford Hotel in Plymouth Road, a wide street leading west. Off this is Canal Road with slate-hung cottages and warehouses on the Wharf at the start of the Tavistock Canal (see chapter 8). The canal passes through The Meadows, a park, to the end of Plymouth Road, where there is a restored fifteenth-century gatehouse and a statue of Sir Francis Drake, who was born at Crowndale a short distance further on. Callington Road climbs out of town past the large Italianate Fitzford church, another Bedford building of the 1860s. Ford and West Streets have some attractive houses and lead back to the centre, where the museum (see chapter 7) is in the town council offices in Drake Street. The north side of town is crossed by a viaduct built in 1890 for the now disused London and South Western Railway. Tavistock had a second railway, the South Devon and Tavistock line, opened from Plymouth in 1859.

TEIGNMOUTH
Early closing Thursday.

Always a port, Teignmouth developed as a resort in the early nineteenth century. The old town is on a spit at the mouth of the Teign estuary and lies south of the railway, which cuts through the town beneath many bridges. The museum (see chapter 7) is near the station, in French Street, which was burnt by the French in 1690. The railway is protected by a sea-wall and promenade as it hugs the coast before turning inland. The Promenade overlooks the beach and pier and has a small grey limestone lighthouse of 1845. Behind are the Den, a grassy park, and the Georgian-period Den Crescent, now mostly hotels. The colonnaded Riviera Cinema is recognisable as the former Assembly Rooms. Powderham Terrace, also facing the sea, is later in date. The narrow and attractive Northumberland Place returns into the town. Off this, New Quay Street leads to New Quay, built in 1820 to convey granite from Dartmoor's Haytor quarries (see chapter 8) for London Bridge. From here there is a view around the curve of the estuary to the docks, always busy with ships exporting clay and importing a variety of goods such as timber. Above the railway, off Exeter Street, St James is a very striking octagonal church of 1820, with a much earlier low tower. St Michael's church near the Promenade is of a similar date, with a Norman-style doorway. To the west of the docks is Bitton Park, where Bitton House is now a council office. The nineteenth-century orangery is sometimes open. Beyond, the long Shaldon Bridge crosses the estuary to Shaldon.

THORVERTON

This pretty village at a meeting of lanes in Devon's red-soil country possesses thatched cottages and houses, cobbled pavements and water channelled through the gutters. The thatched and cob-walled Church House is dated to the fifteenth century. The church (St Thomas à Becket) has a notable fan-vaulted south porch and tall Beer stone piers with angels carved on the capitals. An open-beaked eagle lectern is one of only four in Britain.

TIVERTON

Early closing Thursday; market day Tuesday.
Tiverton gained its wealth as a wool town. The proud Town Hall of 1864 is a centre of focus at the west end of Fore Street, with its octagonal clock-tower and red marble columns. The large St George's church (1714-30) is typical of its period, and between the two buildings is St Andrews Street, which has the Tiverton Museum in an old school (see chapter 7). St Peter Street has the Great House, a Jacobean mansion of about 1613, built for George Slee as a home, business premises and headquarters of the wool trade guild. It is now council offices but parts of it and the garden can be viewed by the public. At his death Slee bequeathed £500 to establish the Slee Almshouses for six poor aged widows or maidens, duly built next door. Slee married Joan Chilcot, whose uncle was Peter Blundell. Her brother Robert founded Chilcot School across the street in 1611. The schoolroom is now a council committee room and the schoolmaster's house a dwelling. Further along the street the Methodist chapel (1814) is a curious combination of red brick and Ionic columns. The beautiful St Peter's church (see chapter 5) is at the north end of the street and owes its fine decoration directly to the wool trade. Beyond is Tiverton Castle (see chapter 4), taken with the town by Sir Thomas Fairfax on

Tiverton town hall.

19th October 1645.
Turning east, Newport Street leads to Bampton Street, which has an old Norman arch next to the Post Office and a Market House with timber colonnades and a clock of 1731. The central part enclosed by these roads has a covered market building with cupola. Gold Street has the Greenway Almshouses and small chapel (1529). Further east and behind a grass court is Old Blundell's School, founded in 1599 by the rich wool merchant Peter Blundell. The building dates from 1604 but the school was moved in 1880 to a spacious site alongside Blundells Road towards Taunton. Canal Hill climbs to the terminus of the Grand Western Canal (see chapter 8).

From the Town Hall Angel Hill drops to the bridge over the Exe to West Exe, which is dominated by John Heathcoat and Company's textile mill (see chapter 8). There is a township of workers' terraced cottages. A surprise in Wellbrook Street is the Walrond Almshouses and chapel, built in 1597 and restored in 1987. A feature is an interesting frieze with carvings and inscription.

TOPSHAM

Once a port for Exeter, Topsham still retains a strong maritime flavour and has some good architecture. There are narrow cross streets off Fore Street, which winds past the church (St Margaret), rebuilt by the Victorians to an unusual cruciform plan. It has a Norman font with a dragon. Memorials include one to Admiral Sir John Duckworth (1817), depicting a white marble bust over a relief of a naval battle. The churchyard has good views across the Exe to the Haldon Hills. There is a copy of a tombstone to Thomas Randle, quartermaster on the *Victory* at Trafalgar, who died in 1851 aged 78. Church House is dated 1385. The Strand continues after Fore Street, with charming eighteenth-century Dutch-style houses close to the water. The museum is here (see chapter 7). Returning close to the shore below the churchyard wall along Ferry Road and Church Causeway, there are more pretty houses including the eighteenth-century Passage Inn and Follett Lodge, the birthplace of the Attorney General Sir William Webb Follett (1798-1845). The Topsham ferry takes foot passengers across the Exe to a point near Topsham Lock on the Exeter Canal (see chapter 8).

TORQUAY
Early closing Wednesday and Saturday.

Torquay is Devon's Riviera, a site with a mild climate and laid out with planned streets and terraces interspersed with gardens, trees and outcropping limestone rocks. There are coastal drives such as Ilsham Marine Drive. Large hotels overlook an attractive coast with enclosed beaches. The place found favour as a resort for naval families during the Napoleonic Wars, when the fleet was stationed in Torbay. Much of the early development of the village of Tor Quay in the later eighteenth century was the work of Sir Robert Palk, and later of the Cary family of Torre Abbey (see chapters 6 and 7). Attention converges on the harbour area with its marina, boat trips and some shipping. Aqualand is an aquarium near Beacon Quay. The green-domed Pavilion next to the Princess Gardens has been converted into a shopping centre and restaurant. The Strand behind the inner harbour has decorated iron pillars supporting a broad covered pavement in front of shops. Overlooking the harbour from the hillside above is St John's church. This and most other churches are strictly Victorian (see chapter 5). Torre Abbey lies to the west of the harbour and is a refreshing reminder of earlier times. It contains a museum and art gallery (see chapters 6 and 7).

The Torquay Natural History Museum (see chapter 7) is in Torwood Street as it climbs from the harbour, and not far beyond in Wellswood are the famous caves at Kents Cavern (see chapter 9). **Babbacombe** is now merged with Torquay. A notorious inhabitant was John Richard Lee, known as 'Babbacombe' Lee, whose death sentence for murder in 1885 was changed to life imprisonment after three failed attempts to hang him. Babbacombe is perhaps best known for its stunning Model Village (see chapter 9), but other attractions include 'Bygones' (see chapter 7). A cliff railway drops 250 feet (76 metres) down a wooded cliff to Oddicombe Beach. St John's church is a notable Victorian piece and **St Marychurch** cannot be mistaken from afar, where the tall tower and spire of its two churches make a prominent landmark (see chapter 5). A pedestrianised shopping street descends gently from the parish church.

TOTNES
Early closing Thursday; market days Tuesday and Friday.

Totnes was once a Saxon town on the west side of the tidal Dart close to its highest navigable point, but the main street now has a mainly Elizabethan and Georgian character. The upper town is dominated by the castle and church tower. Totnes is proud of its heritage and members of the Elizabethan Society dress in period costume once a week during the summer. Near the river The Plains has a granite obelisk to William Wills, a Totnes man who perished on the ill-fated Burke and Wills expedition across the Australian continent in 1861. From here Fore Street climbs up through the town, passing the ancient Brutus Stone set in the pavement on the right-hand side. On the left the Gothic House (1783) is set back and squeezed in Bank Lane. Next, the King Edward VI Grammar School (founded in 1553) is a red-brick Georgian house with a hooded porch and three floors. Number 80 is the Totnes Elizabethan Museum (see chapter 7).

The Eastgate is the entrance to the old walled town and spans the street with a room above. From here Ramparts Walk leads to the Guildhall, a quiet haven on the site of Totnes Priory just north of the church. It is slate-hung, supported by granite pillars, and, inside, the Council Chamber of 1624 is still in regular use. It has panelled seats around the room and historical items on display include Anglo-Saxon coins minted in Totnes in AD 998. One can return to the High Street, which continues above the Eastgate, via the church (see chapter 5). Opposite the church is the timbered house (1585) of Ann Ball, who married Thomas Bodley, founder of Oxford's famous Bodleian Library. Further up the High Street on the right, long colonnades support the slate-hung buildings of the Butterwalk. Across a market square is the modern Civic Hall, also slate-hung. The Devonshire Collection of Period Costume is in Bogan House (see chapter 7). Castle Hill descends to the arch of the North Gate and the entrance to the castle (see chapter 4).

The Dart is spanned by an elegant arched

bridge of 1826, by Charles Fowler. This crosses Vire Island, whose name commemorates a town twinning in 1973, and is now largely bypassed by the new Brutus Bridge further upstream. Across the river is Bridgetown, a mainly Victorian suburb. The Totnes Motor Museum (see chapter 7) and Totnes Heavy Horse Omnibus Centre (see chapter 9) are at Steamer Quay. Boat trips down the scenic Dart estuary to Dartmouth depart from here, and opposite is the Baltic Wharf, where coasters import timber.

UFFCULME
Early closing Thursday.
This large village of pleasant eighteenth- and nineteenth-century houses is on the north side of the Culm valley. Bridge Street descends past the church (see chapter 5) to the river, where an animal-feeds depot and the old railway to a creamery up the valley are reminders that this is agricultural country. In the High Street a prominent old brick brewery building has found a use as the Culm Valley Activities Centre. To the west at Coldharbour, the brick and stone textile mill is now operated as a working museum (see chapter 8).

WESTWARD HO!
Early closing Tuesday.
This resort, established in the second half of the nineteenth century on Bideford Bay, takes its name from Charles Kingsley's famous novel, complete with exclamation mark. Rudyard Kipling was a pupil at the United Services College of 1874, his experiences forming the basis of his book *Stalky and Co.* Midborough House was a music school and chapel to the college. Twentieth-century developments have marred the place but the main asset is the fine beach with a long pebble ridge protecting Northam Burrows (see chapter 2). **Northam** itself has a tall church tower which is a landmark for sailors.

WIDECOMBE-IN-THE-MOOR
Widecombe is famous for Uncle Tom Cobley and the popular fair held here on the second Tuesday in September in the Great Field. Cobley himself came from Spreyton village near South Tawton. The village lies in a valley bottom surrounded by high hills and rocky tors and is striking when approached from the east. The church (St Pancras) has

been called the Cathedral of the Moor. Its tall tower was struck by lightning during a service in 1638 and falling masonry killed four worshippers and injured many others. The colonnaded early sixteenth-century Church House (National Trust) is partly dwelling and partly village hall. Glebe House is of similar date and now a gift shop.

WITHERIDGE
This main-road village with a large market square lies exactly halfway between South Molton and Tiverton. There are thatched and other houses, notably in Fore and West Streets. The church (St John the Baptist) has richly carved stone capitals, font and pulpit. Witheridge has some rough moor to the north and several small hamlets to the south, where **Morchard Bishop** is a hilltop village with good views to Dartmoor and Exmoor and a church with a reconstructed screen of 1490.

WOOLACOMBE
This resort at the north end of Morte Bay has a great sandy beach popular for surfing. Just north is the attractive slate village of **Mortehoe**, its thirteenth-century church with a solid tower, Norman doorways and carved bench ends. Nearby is displayed a salvaged anchor from the SS *Collier*, which ran aground at Rockham Bay in 1914. South past Baggy Point is a smaller beach at Croyde Bay and the village of **Croyde**, where the Gem, Rock and Shell Museum is worth a visit (see chapter 7).

YELVERTON
Early closing Wednesday.
The gateway to Dartmoor and Princetown from Plymouth, Yelverton is a strange place around a large central green. Just south-west are traces of the Harrowbeer airfield, which saw action during the Second World War. Attractions in the vicinity include the Yelverton Paperweight Centre (see chapter 9), Buckland Abbey and the Garden House (see chapter 6) and Burrator Reservoir (see chapter 2). **Meavy** village has an ancient oak on the green and a church with carved Norman stonework. Nearby **Sheepstor** church, in an equally attractive setting beneath the rocky tor, has the graves of Sir James Brooke and his nephew Sir Charles Brooke, Rajahs of Sarawak.

LUNDY

Marisco Castle

ILFRACOMBE

M ▲ I

M   ■ Combe Martin
Once Upon a   ■ *Buzzacott Manor*
Mortehoe   *Time*   *Combe Martin*   ○+ *Parracombe*
Woolacombe   ○ *Bodstone*   *Wildlife Park*
Morte Bay ✳   *Barton*

Hele Mill   *Watermouth Castle*

Heddon's Mouth   *Martinhoe Fortler*   *Valley of Rocks*   *Countisbury*

☐ *Lynton*   ☐
IM *Lynmouth*
Watersmeet

☐ *Chapman Barrows*

☐ *Shoulsbur Castle*

Five Barrows

Chambercombe Manor

▲ *Arlington Court*   ○ *Exmoor Bird Gardens*

Marwood Hill
▲ *Gardens*

■ Braunton
M   *Pilton*

Braunton Burrows ✳

BARNSTAPLE
C M

■ Instow
M ■ Appledore
M ▲ *Tapeley Park*

Northam Burrows ✳
Westward Ho!
Northam
M ■■**C** *Chudleigh Fort*
BIDEFORD

○ *North Devon Farm Park*

Cobbaton Combat
M *Vehicles Museum*

Quince Honey Farm
○
■ **SOUTH**
M MOLTO

Hartland Point ✳
Hartland ▲ Abbey
Clovelly
Hartland Quay ✳**M**
+
Hartland ■
Clovelly Dykes   ○ Buck's Mills
○ *Milky Way*

M ■○ *Big Sheep*

Chittlehampton +

Atherington +

Hancock's Devon Cider

I
Rolle Canal

GREAT TORRINGTON
M ○ *Dartington Crystal*
▲ *Rosemoor Garden*

Gnome
Reserve ○
■
Bradworthy

■ Shebbear

Winkleigh ■

■ Chulmleigh

Morchard Bishop

R. Torridge

■ **HOLSWORTHY**
M

■ Hatherleigh

+ North Tawton

■ Northlew

OKEHAMPTON
C M ■
Sticklepath
Meldon Viaduct **I**
Belstone ✳
Common
South Tawton
MI ■
+
■ South Zeal

Prestonbury Castle

Castle Drogo

Fingle Bridge

Yes Tor ✳
High Willhays ✳

Spinsters' ☐
Rock

+ Stowford
Lewtrenchard +
Lydford
Gorge **C** ✳
Lydford

Gidleigh Castle **C** Chagford
Scorhill Circle ☐
Kestor ☐
Shovel Down Row ☐
Fernworthy Reservoir ✳
Grey Wethers ☐

Cranbro Castle
☐
Moretonhampstea
Miniature
Pony Centre

Bec
Fa

+ Marystow

Brentor +
I *Wheal Betsy*

Great Staple Tor ✳
Plymouth and Dartmoor Railway ✳

Birch Tor ✳
Mine **I** ■
Postbridge ○
Cherry Brook Powder Mills
Powder Mills Forge ○ **I**
I Merrivale

Grimspound ☐
Hameldown ☐
Widecombe-
in-the-Moor ✳

■ Hound
Tor
Haytor ✳

☐ *Foal*
Arish

TAVISTOCK
M ■
Tavistock
Canal **I**

I
Princetown

Wistman's Wood N.R.

R. Tamar

R. Taw

D A R T M O O R
D A R T M N.R.

NORTH DEVON

Old Burrow Fortlet

X M O O R

KEY

* Coast and country (Ch. 2)
⊓ Place of archaeological interest (Ch. 3)
C Castle (Ch. 4)
+ Church (Ch. 5)
▲ Historic building or garden (Ch. 6)
M Museum or gallery (Ch. 7)
I Industrial archaeology (Ch. 8)
O Other places to visit (Ch. 9)
■ Town or village (Ch. 10)

+ Molland

■ Bampton

■ Witheridge

R. Exe

▲ Knightshayes Court
Grand Western Canal
Culmstock
Spicelands +
CM ■ + Uffculme
+ I   C Hemyock
TIVERTON   I
Coldharbour Mill

Cadeleigh +
Devonshire's Centre
Bickleigh Castle ▲ O
Cadbury Castle ⊓▲
Fursdon
Thorverton ■
Silverton +
▲ Killerton
■ CREDITON
+
Newton St Cyres +

■ CULLOMPTON
+

+ Dunkeswell Abbey

■ Broadhembury
⊓ Hembury   ⊓ Dumpdon Great Camp
■ Membury
R. Otter
■ HONITON
M
+ Dalwood Meeting House
Axminster ■
M

Cheriton Bishop

CM▲
I+⊓
EXETER

English Lace School

+ I Broadclyst
Cadhay
Ottery ⊓⊓
St Mary +
Tumbling Weir I
Farway Countryside Park
+ Colyton
Sidbury ⊿ +
Blackbury ⊓ Seaton
Castle   Seaton Tramway
Beer Quarry Caves I
Axmouth *
Dowlands Landslips Nature Reserve

Donkey Sanctuary O
Pecorama O ■ Beer

R. Teign

Exeter Canal I
Topsham ■
M
Woodbury Common
Bicton Park
O M
Branscombe * Beer Head
Mouth
O▲M SIDMOUTH
M Otterton Mill

Blackingstone Rock
Haldon Hill
Woodbury Castle
Lympstone
+ East Budleigh

ner Wood

* Canonteign Falls
Kenton +
A la Ronde
■ Lustleigh   Silverlands
Bovey O ■ Chudleigh
▲ ■ Tracey
arke O
Ugbrooke
Gorse Blossom Miniature Railway
O
* Stover
Bishopsteignton +

Brunel I
Atmos-
pheric
Railway
Dawlish Warren
Nature Reserve

M ▲ ■ Budleigh Salterton
M O
M Country Life Museum
EXMOUTH

M ■ Dawlish

M
TEIGNMOUTH